LEXICON FOR AN AFFECTIVE ARCHIVE

LEXICON FOR AN AFFECTIVE ARCHIVE

Giulia Palladini and Marco Pustianaz

intellect Bristol, UK / Chicago, USA

Note to the English edition

This volume straddles an unusually complex linguistic landscape. One of the very first decisions we took as editors, whose mother tongue is not English (although over the last years we have both written and worked extensively in English), was to give each contributor the chance to write her or his entry in the language of their choosing: be it their mother tongue, or the language which, for practical or affective reasons, they thought would best "belong" to the entry itself.

In approaching the work of revision in preparation for this volume, we have returned to the translated texts with the original versions at hand, wishing — as much as possible — to bridge the gap between the standard variety of English, as we perceived it, and the hybrid linguistic form often resulting from multiple border-crossings. In some cases, we felt the need to intervene rather more substantially on the text delivered by the translator whose name you will see associated with each entry in the Appendix.

With this note, we aim to take full responsibility for such interventions. On the one hand, this will account for the bigger or smaller changes that the translator(s) will find compared to their original texts. On the other, this note is here to acknowledge the often invisible, but utterly material engagement which any act of translation implies as an unfinished business of cultural mediation.

Giulia Palladini and Marco Pustianaz
Berlin / Vercelli, October 2016

CONTENTS

LEXICON FOR AN AFFECTIVE ARCHIVE

Katarzyna Tórz

FOREWORD

The point of departure for this book was the interest shown by the Polish Audiovisual Institute (NInA) in the concept of affective archive, which the editors of this volume, Giulia Palladini and Marco Pustianaz, have been developing and employing in their projects and theoretical reflection since 2010. In 2013, several years after it was founded in order to archive Poland's audio-visual heritage, NInA started searching for a creative and powerful concept that would breathe new life into the way we think about and work with archives, while opening up a perspective that would transcend merely utilitarian or historiographical approaches. This led to an invitation to curate a book that would serve both as an introduction to affect and as a test of its possible applications in the field of archiving. The result is a "counter-lexicon" of sorts: by offering an exploration into the various possible facets of such an archive, this book intends to inspire and invite the reader to take part in a multi-layered encounter.

The process of making this book involved not only encounters with people and archives, but also with ideas about archiving itself—a practice that profoundly shapes our contemporary world, engages it in dialogue and argument, and forces us to take a position. The tangible form taken by this lexicon is a natural consequence of the processual nature of its compilation and creation. The selected authors were asked to propose an entry or design a visual intervention in a form of their own choosing. All content, written in the author's language of choice, is published here for the first time in English. Thus, the lexicon contains pieces that have been animated by an attitude of mindfulness, both at a conceptual stage and in the process of reaching their final form: they share an awareness of becoming a new archive by being archived in the lexicon, and a focused attention not only on their objects, but also on the context in which their affect would come to rest.

By giving authors and artists from different countries, contexts, and cultures the opportunity to meet in the pages of the book, this curatorial approach resembles the process of putting together an exhibition, where the conceptual element intertwines with the personalities of every participant, and is further compounded by the element of surprise involved in commissioning new work. The lexicon encourages its readers to experience archives in a special and intimate way: to approach them at close range, to take a stance on the worlds they are opening up. Similarly to the items displayed at an exhibition, the entries in this book have been arranged in a carefully ordered fashion according to a path chosen by the curators. However, the choice of how to explore the lexicon is up to the reader: she can open it at random, examine its multiple facets, re-read favourite entries, while leaving others for later inspection or even skipping them.

We hope that the lexicon will spark an interest in the relationship between archive and affect among researchers, artists, and viewers. Archives transcend the boundaries of specializations, disciplines, and social groups; they shape our own identities and the way we think about history; they are often the chance outcome of singular life stories, while at the same time shaping the collective layers of culture. This means that the phenomenon requires a constant critical examination. Archives also pose a challenge to institutions, whose task it is to adopt the best archival practices for proper storage and presentation, while also addressing contemporary sensibilities.

This lexicon is the result of the combined efforts of many people: curators, writers, editors, and translators. Several years in the making, this project would not have been possible without the openness to interdisciplinary approaches on the part of the participating institutions. Each of them, in their own way, is interested in broadening the spectrum of debate and the perception of the archive as an important field of study—an area of fascinating artistic exploration and a crucial factor in how we as humans are rooted in the world: NInA and słowo obraz/terytoria (the co-publishers of the Polish version of the book), Intellect (the publisher of the English version you are reading now), the University of Roehampton's Department of Drama, Theatre and Performance (which has generously co-financed the project), and Live Art Development Agency (which has sponsored the development of this project and supported its transnational life).

Giulia Palladini and Marco Pustianaz

THE MAKING OF OUR *LEXICON*

Adieu. Welcome.

Introductions are often written at the end, when the book that is just beyond their threshold has in fact already been written. Therefore, they resemble more the words of an adieu. The book is being archived, packed up, and closed. On the other hand, this is perhaps the first time when we, as its curators, glimpse the existence of our book as such, now that it is taking the shape that will distinguish it from all the others. For the first time the book knows that the time has come. We settle our accounts with what has been gathered inside, ready to close the gates, so that they can be opened again.

The movements of closure and opening—mimicked by your turning the pages again and again—are folded one into the other, like the recto and verso of a page. What holds them together is the temporary absence of reading that is filled up with a suspended breath, a tiny affect of a hand moving, of eyes remembering and anticipating. Nothing is ostensibly happening, yet this is one moment of decision, of eventful suspension. You are the agents of time, the harbingers of a new arkhè, or beginning. You are treating the archive as though it had not yet been closed. By doing so you become capable of turning it against itself. There will be no rest in this archive, now that you have come.

The beginning of a description

Our *Lexicon* is a collection of encounters with archives and archival materials—an encounter understood as an affective and critical practice involved in the construction of memory. This book offers glimpses into the intimate relation born out of the experience of finding, accessing, remembering, or, indeed, imagining and creating an archive. Such an archive may be institutional, public, private, or still in the making, perhaps wished-for, bordering on the imaginary and the impossible.

The volume, encompassing contributions by 25 different authors, is organized into entries, each introduced by a simple keyword, as you would find in a lexicon. Each entry represents a singular account (a "story") testifying to the affective, political, and intellectual challenges posed by individual and collective memories. The authors featured in the book cover a wide range of relations with archival practices: they are involved in archives either as professionals, artists, engaged participants, researchers, writers, curators, or in many of these roles rolled into one.

Differently from a standard lexicon, however, this book does not attempt to present an accomplished, unified body of knowledge regarding its topic: each entry gives a particular access to the scope and resonance of a concrete archival *exemplum*. In other words, each entry is both a story and a reflection on the way the author has chosen to address the question of the archive itself. The format of each contribution is likewise various: the book encompasses short narrative essays, personal meditations, visual artworks, performance materials, and other kinds of creative compositions. The only restriction imposed on the authors was brevity: each story is concentrated in a few pages and is intended to offer a glimpse into a much broader horizon, in time, space, and thought.

The use of keywords

In our *Lexicon* the keywords function as a double, Janus-like vector of time: they point to a past as well as to a future use. In the beginning, as we started conceiving the book, they served as orientation to the authors, a signpost to trace a route along the winding paths of his or her memory. The choice of keyword and topic developed at the same time, reinforcing one another. Starting with a specific archive in mind, each author was asked to select a word that conveyed its affective core. In turn, once the keyword appeared, it fed back into the composition of each entry, giving it a centre of gravity, a *body*. Now that the book has taken shape, the keywords remain as both a reminder of, and a passageway to, each archive, marking the space between author and reader. The pages where the keywords are placed are thresholds where reading is delayed; each keyword becomes an echo chamber reverberating with its past operation, now amplified by the resonances you are bringing to it.

At a certain point—maybe with a slight surprise—you will find some blank pages where you can mark *your own* keyword: here you are given the space and time to take stock of the affects gathered in your reading. Imagine this space as a resting space in your ramble: you are taking a walk passing from one spot to the next, you sit down on a bench, at the crossroads of a public path. You may write, draw, doodle … or just enjoy the whiteness, full of potential, of these pages, then move on, leaving them behind until your next return.

How this book became an affective archive

By eschewing the neutral randomness of alphabetical order, the present trail of keywords gives shape to a constellation linking one archive to the other. An important part of our curatorial work went into tracing our chosen path by following the associations, the points of contact or conflict that unexpectedly emerged while we experimented with the effects of different orderings.

By way of an extended process of montage and composition, this book became for us a *habitat*, a lived environment. The longer we dwelt in it, the more relations of proximity started to emerge beyond our own initial expectations. As soon as we started thinking about proximity or distance, as soon as we accepted the challenge to pursue and reshuffle the multiple and ambivalent affects released by the collected encounters, we realized that our *Lexicon* had become in its turn an affective archive.

We had embraced the pleasure of engaging with the composition of its internal echoes on the stage of our paper theatre: a magic lantern superimposing our own mode of encounter with a collection of other people's archival encounters. Our *Lexicon* is the result of this double motion: our own affective movement inserted into the affective movement of the archives that we had collected. This is why we present this *Lexicon* not as a collection *of* archives but as a praxis striving towards, as well as working *for*, an affective archive.

Ours is only one of many possible trails: the reader is invited to shape her own different route, create different constellations of archives, as well as insert one of her own. The static nature of the lexicon, traditionally used as a reference tool characterized by sufficiency, is intentionally rejected by embracing insufficiency and movement as the book's structural elements. Incomplete by design as a lexicon, it is therefore fully complete as an affective archive.

Rather than a concept, *affective archive* names for us a horizon, a limit, a possibility always ready to be enacted and released in every archive. Seen as a process of memory-making in which everybody is involved—producing the scene of our common, yet also divided, dwelling space—the affective archive wavers between materiality and immateriality, between conservation and transformation. Ultimately, the hybrid term *affective archive* is intended to acknowledge the impulse that both creates and mobilizes the archive as an endless process. Speaking of affective archives, therefore, makes us partly responsible for the yet unknown directions of our own archiving, acknowledged as a vector of transformation.

Once you see affect moving in the archives, there is no longer any rest within them. This can be both a source of terror and delight, as we shall see in the next story.

A tale of fire and books

François Truffaut's film *Fahrenheit 451* (1966) tells the wonderful story of a community: the community of the *hommes-livres*. They are free (*livres*), yet at the same time castaways in a society where the act of reading is considered a crime: playing on the double meaning of the French word *livres*, Truffaut turns the book lovers into *free men* who decide to become human *books*. Each has learned by heart the text of a favourite book, banished by law and destroyed by fire. Though physically burnt by the regime's Firemen, each of these books is thus held virtually—*in potentia*—in their bodies. By means of their wondrous technology of memory, the "book-men" take refuge in the forest, getting ready for the moment when someone will care to *browse* them, when someone will care to listen to what they are able to repeat.

In this tale each book is turned into a walking body, and vice versa: each body is turned into a walking book, just like Guy Montag, a fireman now become book-lover, who chooses to archive in his memory Edgar Allan Poe's *Tales of Mystery and Imagination*. In a stunning act of revolt, the readers turn themselves into the physical support of the books by now destroyed, each word burning in their memory so that they can mumble, mouth, and spit their content like a flame. Their mission is to ensure the survival of each individual archive through repeated chains of transmission.

We are opening up our *Lexicon* with this story, because it shows the emergence of an affective archive embodied by a new community defined by archival practice. The books are archived in, and as, bodies, made to live once again, both in the encounter with a listener and in solitary, intimate repetitions of passages. These oral performances are both acts of memory and desire. What they hold in store is the distilled memory of a desire not only to read—a desire that fired the need to preserve the book in the first place—but also to pass it on despite all odds. Through the trauma of loss, a radical desire is released, with a paradoxical liberation that coincides with their exile. This story is both a tale of terror and one of *jouissance*.

A tale of terror. Or, archive by fire (Marco Pustianaz)

By conflating multiple references to utter destruction—from the burning of the Library of Alexandria to the Nazi burnings of books—*Fahrenheit 451* plays on the intimate bond between terror and archive. In order to produce the urgency of an archival community literally rising like a phoenix from the ashes, this tale has to stage the terrifying horizon of a holocaust, "a complete burning." As books perish amid the flames, bodies take the task to become their new vessel and support.

Two lessons may be drawn from this tale of conversion. Firstly, if a body can become an archive, it is only because the body is already a living archive. Secondly, if an archive can be turned into a body, the fantasy of closure inherent in archival conservation is already compromised. In effect, once tied to a body, the archive is tied up with the history of that body, implying becoming and mortality. The book's legacy embodied in the *hommes-livres*, for example, has also become fatally mortal, measured by their human lifespan. Embodiment brings to the fore the precariousness

A tale of delight. Or, *jouissance d'archive* (Giulia Palladini)

In the last scene of *Fahrenheit 451*, we witness the body-to-body transmission of one of the books archived by the *hommes-livres*: *The Weir of Hermiston* by Robert Louis Stevenson. An old man is standing on a deathbed arranged in a forest, on the shore of a small lake, warmed up by a fire. He is covered with a black coat, a young boy sitting at his side, quietly listening. The man, whose name has become *The Weir of Hermiston*, is "reciting himself" so that his grandson can in turn become the book: the child first listens, then patiently repeats the passages, in no hurry, as a habit that the two have seemingly been sharing for a while, as a rehearsal for a moment to come. The child is learning the book by heart, in order to pass it on, to keep alive the embodied knowledge of the dying man for a time when the evidence of his bodily existence has disappeared from the world.

We might imagine that the child has never actually "read" *The Weir of Hermiston*; that his own experience of reading, having grown up among the *hommes-livres*, ignores the attachment to the materiality of books felt of any archive's closure. Conservation is carried forward, yet is also undermined by transmission, which implies translation and change, in other words, loss.

It may be paradoxical to link archives with loss. Yet, an archive is defined by its own partiality, which stands for everything else that has been lost: it is a synecdoche, a part for the whole. This is only the first of many archival duplicities: archives, even though presumed to stand against loss, are themselves born out of it. By emerging from loss, they somehow also represent it. As if what is not there lent the archive its power to show and speak. The affective archive of the *hommes-livres* has to do with mourning, an active mourning, since it impels the invention of a new technology: embodiment.

As a consequence of its embodiment, the archive ceases to have a domicile and is forced to embrace nomadism and migration. It also loses any pretence of sufficiency: its survival is not guaranteed, but is entrusted to the chance agency of other bodies who choose to take up its affective potential and become its new archiving impulse. And so on and on, because

by those who initiated this community. After it has been learnt by heart, each book reaching the forest where the *hommes-livres* hide gets burnt, eliminating all evidence of its bodily existence in the world: only thus will it never again run the risk of disappearing.

The image of the child consigning the book to memory resembles that of a spectator arrived too late on the scene of history—the past in which that particular book had materially existed. At the end of the film, he takes over the narrative and continues reciting the book to the dead body of the old man, who, like the protagonist of his beloved Stevenson's novel, dies "as he thought he would, while the first snows of winter fell". The child is handed both the product and the memorability of someone else's attachment. He is, like many of us, consigned the burden and delight of his grandfather's legacy, but this kind of belonging entails a technology of archiving as well. The survival of this technology in the bodies of those who are going to archive the first generation of *homme-livres* reproduces the bizarre duality of survival (as embodied praxis) and disappearance (as materiality) that characterizes the destiny of books in the science-fiction future first imagined by Ray Bradbury and later re-staged by François Truffaut.

one instance of successful transmission is never enough; it needs an endless chain of bodies that might at any time fail to link up.

It is important to stress the attachment to the technology of this particular transmission, in order to better understand how a private attachment to an individual book can translate into the social foundation of a community. Maybe what is tragic is not just the loss of any specific book—this would be a sentimental reading of the freemen's affect—but the even more terrible danger of losing the singular connectivity experienced through the technology that has shaped their attachment in the first place. Losing a technology means the loss of all connections enabled by it. The response of the *hommes-livres* will be to displace that technology, translating utter loss into exodus or exile.

The impulse by which the archive is subjected to the trauma of displacement may be called its affect. Affect neither belongs to the archive nor to its future carriers; it neither names the latter's decision to become the archive's destiny, nor a quality inherent in the archive *per se*. Affect names the linkage by which their (imaginary) conversion becomes possible: it is the hyphen turning each *homme* into the hybrid identity called *homme-livre*.

To a certain extent, in the uneasy position of the child as "latecomer spectator" (echoing a beautiful expression by Joe Kelleher) and in the demand placed upon him to handle the continuation of a particular memory, we could also recognize the plight of any researcher in front of archival materials. In any encounter with the materiality of a disappeared past, what is at stake is the complex responsibility of taking care of an impossible survival; similarly, in imagining how *to pass on* what is left for us to receive, there is at stake a distinctive restlessness of affects, demanding not only further transmission, but also a particular politics of use involved in the passing on of any memory.

The glimmering horizon that we call *affective archive*, in which I have inscribed the narrative of this story, names the always latent possibility to think of memory as something other than a series of traces: mine is a desire to reconfigure memory as a praxis produced always in a landscape of radical discontinuity with the past, and even with the future. The logic of the affective archive resists the stasis of consignment: it names the movement that both accumulates and organizes what can be spoken again, in its intrinsic multiplicity, in its forms of appearance going beyond the sole

In this tale, an explicit connection is made between trauma, affect, and technology. As a result, the *hommes-livres* become transmitting machines, whose attachments blur the boundary between political and psychic life: they become their own technology.

Archives and bodies are also implicated through repetition and disruption. Without repetition there would be no effect of continuity and persistence; without disruption there would be no dislocation and passage. In our tale, transmission originates as a response, as an impulse to avert oblivion, destruction, and obliteration—the negative obverse of its positive drive. The ardent desire of the *hommes-livres* hovers on the horizon between life and death, the slippery location of every archive. In an essay by Shoshana Felman bearing the title "Fire in the Archive," she has concisely renamed death as "forgetfulness": "There would be no archive without the possibility (the danger) of forgetfulness." The act of archiving stands as an attempt to avert or infinitely delay what we know is inevitable: the fragility of connections and their continuous loss.

Archives are sites where our relation with historicity becomes deeply enmeshed with affect and trauma. The traumatic horizon of loss impels

domain of value—at least, a value deemed as objectively measurable. An affective archive is both the deposit, the habitat, and the means of production of historical potentiality.

Indeed, in *Fahrenheit 451* any one body, including the child's, is serving not only as a temporary memory support. One day each *homme-livre*—or at least so they imagine in their utopian vision—will be called upon to reproduce, once again, the books that had been made to disappear. Not only will the books, one day, be printed again, but also the archiving technology invented by the *hommes-livres* (or retrieved from an obliterated past) will be handed over to other book lovers, as a tactics to be deployed when future moments of danger occur. In a sense, the political project of transmitting such technology also involves the secret encoding of possibilities of resistance: *how to turn yourself into an affective archive.*

It is reasonable to imagine, on the other hand, that the child will also want to make other uses of such memory in the future. Perhaps the child will forget some of Stevenson's words, and become attached to other, invent other words, or group them differently – playing with their montage, their composition, their order. We might imagine the words of *The Weir of* a dislocation, an exodus. Traumas are productive sites of future history, especially as their import and meaning is not available immediately, but *goes underground* as a deferred, delayed effect. History, as Cathy Caruth has argued, "is precisely the way we are implicated in each other's traumas." We are "implicated," not just involved but also enmeshed, entangled in so intimately that it is no longer possible to tell apart inside and outside, the cause and the effect. As a result, traumas cease to be our own, they become "each other's." They are archived through the embodied linkage of affect.

The social effect produced by such linkages is shown by the freemen's community, who have literally walked through the fire of trauma to institute a new beginning with their archival act. Whether they can faithfully remember their book is perhaps of secondary importance; even if they could, we know that their affective archive is a product of loss anyway (of a specific materiality, for instance). What is crucial, rather, is that, having consigned their bodies to the archive, they now belong to it in a radically different way. They belong to it by belonging each to the other: their belonging has begun again with an archival act. Hence the institutional or foundational nature of archives: they posit, albeit silently, a beginning.

Hermiston as they become part of a constellation with other words, both in his memory and in the liberated future in which books will be printed again; we might imagine, too, this new constellation encountered in turn by other newborn bodies, other archiving subjectivities. On the other hand, it might be the child's own affective archiving that suggests the intimate necessity connecting Stevenson's words, and distinguishes them from the random accumulation of any other words: we might imagine that this would happen not so much as a gesture of loyalty, but as an inventive act of memory.

We might wish that the child, on recalling one day the early moment of transmission on his grandfather's deathbed, would also remember the joy of reading that had long before imprinted its mark on the utopian project of the *homme-livres* and nourished their labour of renewal. We might wish that the sparkle of this joy would be mobilized for other forms of renewal, impressing other forms of attachment on the unlimited surface of the future. We might dream about this child as an artist working with memory, playing with history as though with creative matter, and approaching his own archiving as an act of making, a re-production outside the lineage of filiation.

As Derrida suggested in *Archive Fever*, archives have little to do with preserving the past. They are there to launch a future. In the archive, we never encounter the past but only what remains of it, after the fire. Yet, those poor remainders are produced retrospectively by our encounter with the archive to become the foundation of what we will have been, of what we are now. From so little, so much. That is part of the terror in the archive.

We might finally figure this child as a spectre of a certain *jouissance d'archive*: a lightness of memorability and renewal, an act of choice and courage participating in the singular and collective encounter with a certain habitat of memory, with the forms of appearance and metamorphosis that constantly shape and transform our own idea of archiving.

Alessandra Violi

BOXES

After you died, your photographs and other bits of your past life—pictures of your dad and mum, your mother's will written by hand on a skin-like piece of paper, scraps of an old advert for Siderexport showing dad smiling among his colleagues, a hair clip made to look like an improbable flower—all ended up in a box.

It's funny how we all become curators when dealing with the belongings of our ghosts, literally *taking care* of their objects by enclosing them in a case or a casket, the box as a safe that is meant to preserve what is precious, the unnumbered lots of our private archive. Come to think of it, though, this boxing is as mortifying as storing items in those filing cartons used for public archiving: the box can be a coffin from which no retrieval is expected; lifeless things may lie there in waiting, but their concealment is, in fact, an intimation of their disappearance, of their social and affective death.

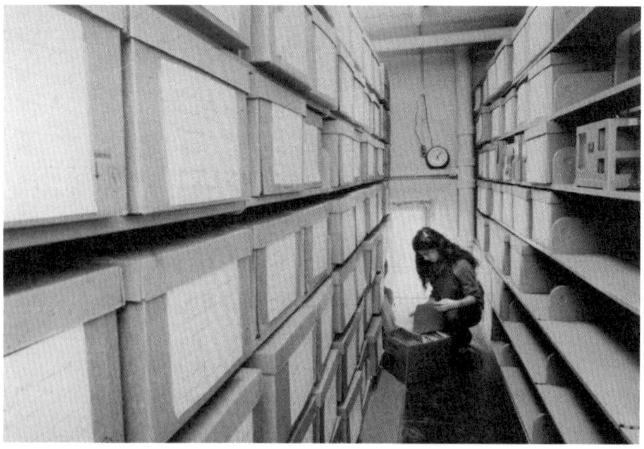

I now realize that this is probably why I treated your coffin as if it were a box of a different kind. One of those Cornellian boxes full of toy-like objects and flotsam, faded photographs, marbles, pins, grains of sand and other trivia, all gathered there to perform some secret task. Joseph Cornell imagined them as the homes of ballerinas, opera singers and movie actresses, female performers who would replay the contents of his boxes in endless combinations through their bodies: dancing, acting, fading like the human voice; a deathly box turned into a living stage and a theatre-box for us, the absent witnesses of their performances. I have often written about Cornell's boxes in my academic work, understanding (through the lens of Walter Benjamin) that his queer cases full of ticky-tacky were themselves archives of another sort—the box creating a third, intermediate space where material things stopped being dead relics of the world outside or tokens of the affective world inside, but rather cross-indexed each other to perform new constellations and surprising conversations. An entry in Cornell's diary thus wondered what the objects randomly integrated in his boxes "would have to say to each other," reinventing the box as an archive of virtualities, a Pandora's box generating potentialities.

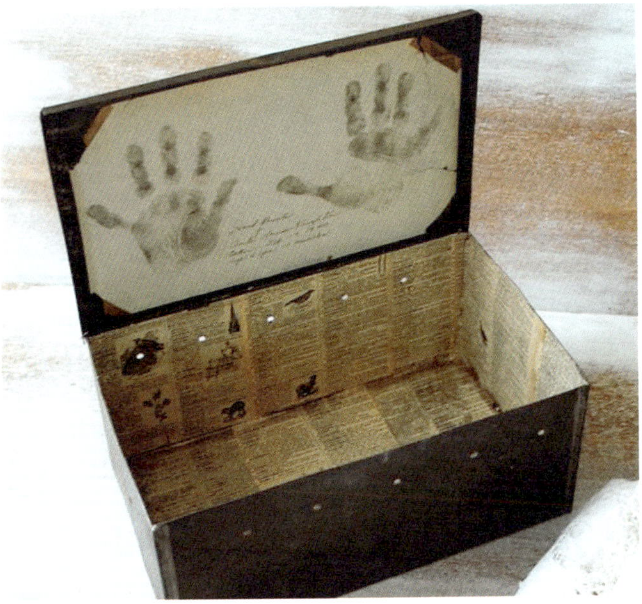

Joseph Cornell's diary, January 4th, 1943:
"Every so often pieces turn up—and the thing is clearing up but the clues are so many that I am glad this mystery will never be entirely so (cleared). Of the sailor's box from the trunk other inhabitants get out something every so often."

As your box had to be closed and sealed off, what I had studied for my job percolated through my nerves and became simply an affective impulse acted out by the body (my gesture was indeed secretive, as if unconsciously aware of transgressing some conventional—if not sacred—function of the wooden coffer): I slipped, next to your unresponsive face, a senseless piece of ribbon and an old photo of you and dad, one of those tacky holiday souvenirs where the sun shines so shamelessly that the light looks unreal. Admirers of Joseph Cornell claim that his boxes are best appreciated by putting them on the floor and lying next to them. His boxes invite you to *play* dead—Cornell got his idea of boxing things from Houdini, the famous escape artist who could flee the encasement of death—or to stop being straight and be nothing but an affected body, whether in rest or sleep, intimacy or disease—Cornell got his idea of boxing things from the miniature toys he made for his brother Robert, who suffered from cerebral palsy. Perhaps my nesting of an archive within another was an exchange of gifts, as I can't really tell now whether the box was meant for you, filling it with things you could replay with while lying, or for me, staging your death in my memory as a theatre of endless performances and affective animations.

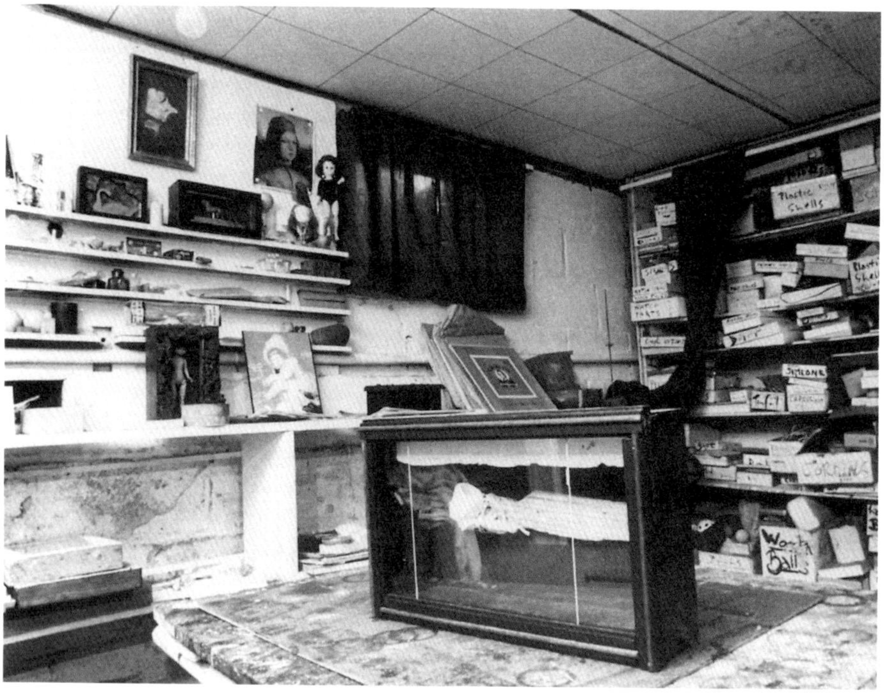

Then other boxes came. Those into which I had to pack all my belongings for moving out, choosing to go back to the house where I had grown up and where you had lived until the end. Against the advice of some of my friends not to take residence in a mausoleum, afraid that I would turn myself into a document of our shared past, I felt that "home" could be re-enacted differently, its repository of gestures and rituals fleshed out as new events. The living box of the body against dead repetition in the "little box" of our house.

♪ ♫ ♬

> "Little boxes on the hillside, little boxes made of ticky-tacky. Little boxes on the hillside, little boxes all the same. There's a green one and a pink one and a blue one and a yellow one. And they're all made out of ticky-tacky and they all look just the same."

♪♫♬

Around the year that I was born, Malvina Reynolds sang about people being serialized in "little boxes," homes and workplaces packaging life stories into the same imitation game. So, the word "ticky-tacky," which she invented for the purpose, is about my age, an item of a musical archive that I can now play differently. You can't imagine the amount of ticky-tacky I had to sort out while moving here, boxing in and boxing out heaps of trivia and memorabilia, fingering each of them: grandmother's old-fashioned lace gloves, stray pieces of cloth ("what the hell…?"), a diary from the time of World War II by a grandfather I never knew, buttons, my first sketchbook that you had religiously kept in a drawer. My archive, your archive, and at each turn around the home-box that my body knew by heart a strange feeling of déjà-vu, but made new, enacting a different story. The making of an archive is in the pulse between keep and throw, but Cornell gave me a knack for the discarded: ping-pong balls, hair pins, feathers … he stored them away in 57 cartons that now make up the artist's archive at the Smithsonian American Art Museum. He never meant them as collectibles, though. The point was to give them new homes, out of the archive-box into his art boxes, what he called "toys" for affective games with the past, recounting a history that never was except in the imagination of the player.

That's how I have learnt that boxes are not for storing the belongings of ghosts, but for ghosting time: like your old hatbox that now contains your archive, my affective processes are neither of the past nor of the present. They hover out of (the archive's) order, inhabiting a space of transition just like this letter, left in this post-box for no future collection.

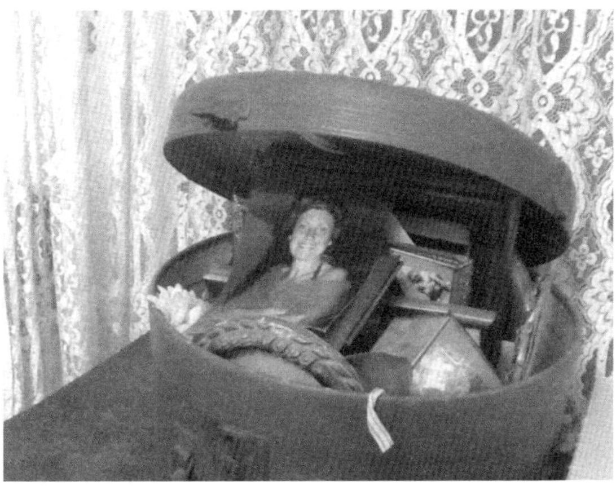

Cornell's diary, March 20th, 1956:
"flavour vs mere cataloguing *aftermath* * of yesterday a superb moment pulling the box of Cerrito material from under bed—after months of inattention sense of vintaging, as last look also months ago—in garage at similar GC44 material—stuffing of boxes from closet to cellar […] player in the kitchen"

Kateřina Šedá

VNUČKA

GRANDDAUGHTER

Once upon a time

When I was little, neither of my grandmothers ever played with me. Birthdays or Christmas get-togethers were the only occasions we would see each other regularly. Strangely enough, as a child I didn't mind it so much, but later I realized that I didn't know either of my grandmothers too well. I never felt like forcing the issue, so in time I just got used to things. Then, in 2005, a turning point came and things started to change.

My grandmother Jana (1939–2007) decided that after retiring she would put an end to all her activities and from one day to the next she stopped doing anything at all. At first, I told myself the main reason for her resignation must have been my grandfather's death, but she disabused me of that notion: "At last I don't have to cook anymore!" Of course, his death affected her, but, at the same time, it gave her the pretext to do nothing whatsoever. She would only get up out of bed to eat lunch, which my mother would prepare for her; she stopped doing housework, cooking, and shopping. Her favourite household member became the TV, which she was capable of watching non-stop all week. *It doesn't matter* was the phrase she'd use most often in answer to most of our questions. So, even though she was healthy and able to fend for herself, we were forced to do absolutely everything for her, including making decisions.

That was what led me to try and engage her in activities that might open up topics of conversation for us. From the very first, I ruled out all household chores, as they represented a kind of punishment for her. I noticed that she tended to live in the past rather than in the present, so that's where I zeroed in. One of the few things she kept returning to was the 33 years she'd been in charge of tool stocks in a store that sold household goods in Brno (1950–1983). She still remembered over 650 items, including their prices. On that basis, it occurred to me to try and reconstruct the store, on paper at least, and get her back to work. The different items she started to draw at my bidding became the main subject of conversation for our entire family.

Eventually, I added other activities to the drawing so my grandmother would stay motivated throughout the day. First thing in the morning, we'd do *What's it for?*, an exercise in which I'd ask her what all sorts of things were for and she'd answer on paper. At first, I didn't place too much importance on this "warm-up," but in time it turned out to perfectly illustrate my grandmother's view of the world and her way of thinking. The slightest thing would have some significance or purpose, but she herself was, in her own words, GOOD FOR NOTHING. Every city in the world was *for living in*, but all that Brno, where we live, was good for was producing tractors. Each day before lunch I'd do *1× daily before meals*, an exercise in which I'd give my grandmother a questionnaire to fill in before we ate. It was a way of leading into a conversation over lunch, but at first it didn't work at all. She'd just fill in the questionnaire and then start reading. After a while, I realized my grandmother would only talk when one of the questions didn't make sense. So I started filling the questionnaires with nonsensical questions like "If your dog wore clothing, how would you dress him?" Over two years I got to ask her several thousand questions and was at least able to get to know her a bit better that way.

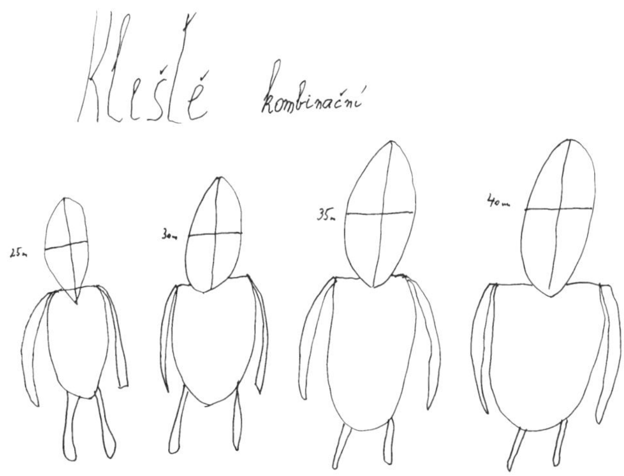

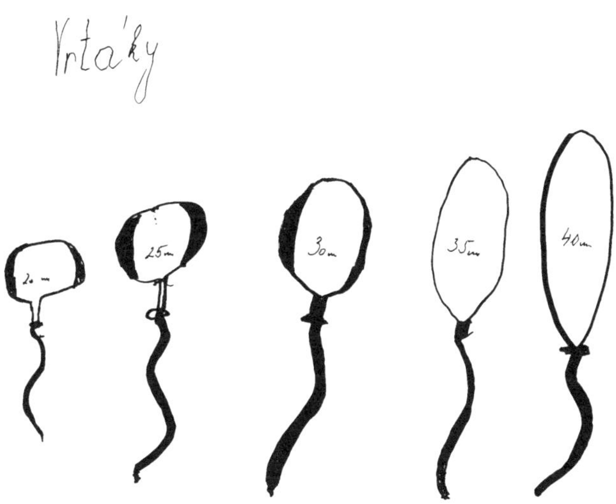

Whereas my grandmother Jana and I really got quite close in the course of our activities, my grandmother Milada (1935–) remained as distant as she'd ever been. Paradoxically, her problem was quite the opposite—she'd never ever take a rest. When she retired she seemed to become even more active than before—she'd regularly go to work in the garden with my grandfather Mílo and would always say the two of them were self-sufficient. When he died in 2006, my grandmother bravely went on "functioning" as before. I always admired her for that and my admiration distracted me from the fact that thanks to her bustling activity I'd never really got to know her.

In 2009, my daughter Julie was born and within four weeks my husband had left us. I fell into a funk, but my family quickly pulled me out of it. My parents helped me, and sometimes my grandmother Milada would come and take care of little Julie. Once I noticed she was trying to recount a convoluted classical fairy tale and I asked her to tell her about her own life instead. She looked at me, surprised: "My own life? Nothing's happened in my life! I've had a completely normal life." Then it occurred to me that she might write a children's book for Julie about her life and thereby bridge the gap that separated us.

At first, my grandmother didn't want to—she doesn't like writing or drawing. She said she'd rather be ploughing a field. Yet, she eventually set about writing and drawing anyhow, and her text surprised us all. She divided the resulting book, titled *Normal Life*, into five basic chapters ("Not Much of a Childhood," "I Got Married," "We Had a Good Life," "We Were Creating a New Society," and "Life's Halfway Point"), which captured the important moments of her life. She devoted the greatest details to her childhood, during which she had to work a lot, so she was actually glad when it was over. Most of her personal life took place in communist Czechoslovakia and in her words, "Things were better then." She described the certainties of the time and made a comparison with life today through both writing and illustrations.

After the revolution in 1989, a lot of things changed here. The government changed and the regime changed to this so-called capitalism we have now. Interpersonal relationships also changed. People were now able to travel abroad, like they'd always wanted to before the revolution but many of them couldn't afford to anyhow. We've got democracy here, but many people interpret it in whatever way suits them; they think they can do whatever they want, but often that's not the case (you have to respect law and order). Today it's all mainly about money and property because our economy has basically collapsed. People don't have jobs and so they don't have money for housing and often for culture either. People have stopped going to the movies and the theatre because they're beyond their means. Money comes first. A lot of families are living in debt they can't pay back and so they end up having their property and often even their houses seized. Since 1989 there have been a lot of homeless people and beggars here. There's a lot of stealing going on. Drugs and murder have also become rampant. Our moral fibre has weakened significantly; every second marriage ends in divorce and few children are born—people are afraid they won't be able to support them. You also see a surge in diseases you didn't see before (tuberculosis, among others)—that's also due to migrations of people coming here for work and a better life. Agriculture is also doing really poorly. Land has been returned to the original owners, but they aren't able to work it so a lot of fields are left uncultivated and we end up importing a lot of foods that are of a lower quality than if we'd grown them ourselves. In the past our agriculture was heavily state-subsidized, but today there's no money for that anymore. Also, not much housing is being built and what is being built is relatively expensive. Many houses have been returned to the original owners who then impose rents people can't afford (mainly the elderly and families with small children). There are all sorts of goods in stores, mainly imported, but they're often so overpriced that a lot of people can't afford them. Almost everything is imported—clothing, consumer goods (from electronics to cars) and food, which is often of poor quality—whereas local vegetables, fruits and other foods are looked down upon and thrown away. In 1989, people occupied the squares to jingle their keys and expected the world to be upended. A lot of them didn't even know why they were there. A lot of things have gone downhill since then.

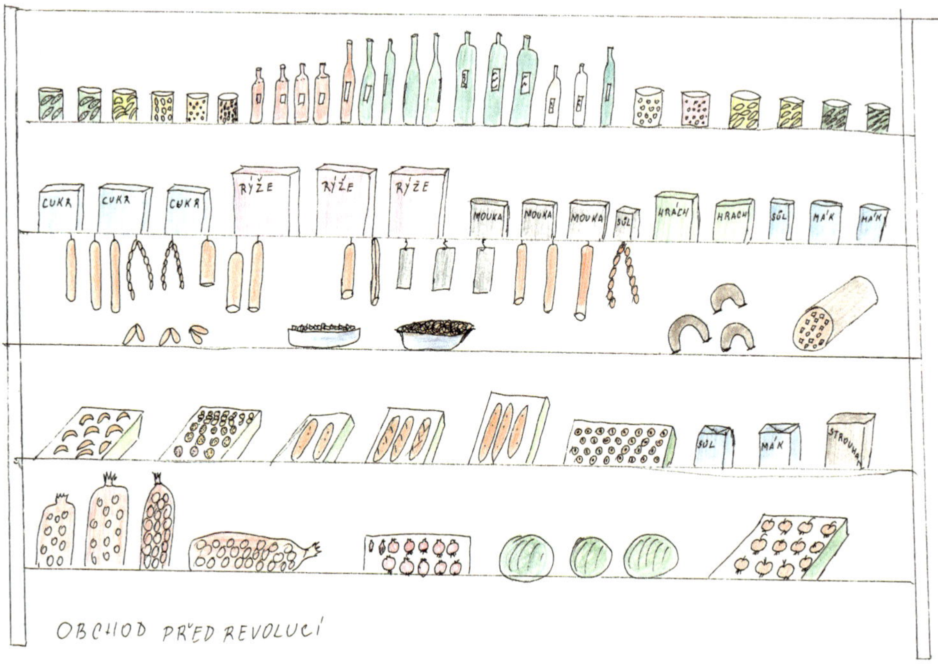

OBCHOD PŘED REVOLUCÍ

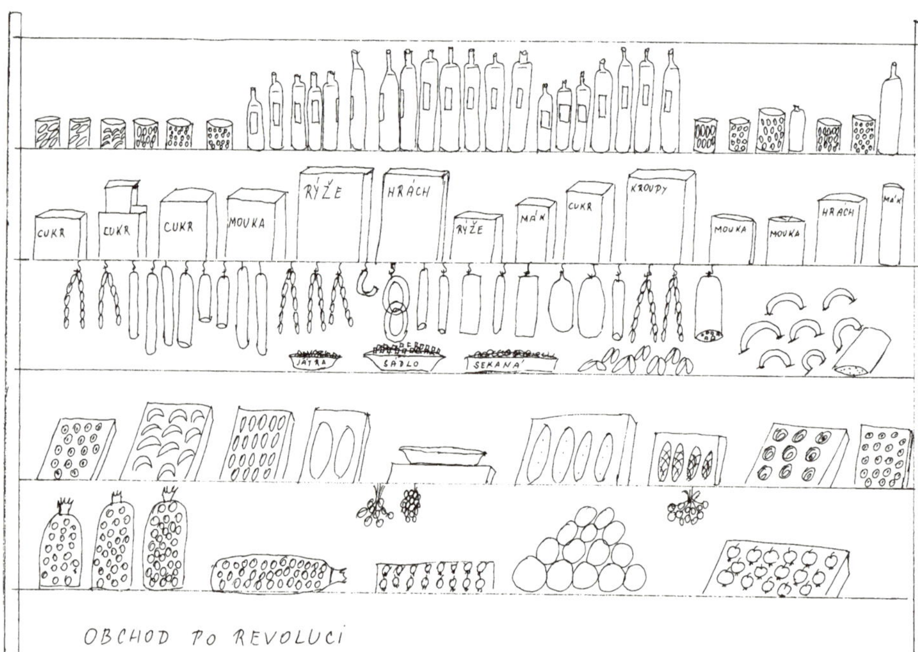

OBCHOD PO REVOLUCI

That's how my grandmother describes her view of history, which is in sharp contrast to what children can read in textbooks today. However, her story is typical of the accounts of numerous Czech grandmothers who are still telling their stories behind the closed doors of their homes.

Dorota Krakowska

KRES

LIMIT

zostać wygnany	גָּלָה	płacz	בְּכִיָּה, בְּכִיָּה—יוֹת
modlitwa	תְּחִנָּה—נּוֹת	patrzył	הִבִּיט

1) **Zadanie**: Przepisać wszystkie czasowniki z ustępu 80. z עָבָר na עָתִיד w tej samej formie i liczbie.

Lekcya LXXXI.

dosyć	דַּי	powiedz!	הַגִּידִי !
najdroższy—a	יַקִּיר—רָה	wdziera się	מִתְפָּרֵץ
wybrany, ulubieniec	בָּחִיר	zachodni	מַעֲרָבִי
na wieki	לְעוֹלָמִים	psalmy	תְּהִלִּים
kres, przyszłość	אַחֲרִית	błaga, ubłaga	מַפִּיל תְּחִנָּה
konieczny, potrzebny—a	נָחוּץ, נְחוּצָה	idzie	מְהַלֵּךְ (הוֹלֵךְ)
mnożyć się	רָבָה	przełom, rozpadlina, rys	פֶּרֶץ, פְּרָצִים
wypędzą	יְגָרְשׁוּ	ach!	הָהּ !
wykorzenić	שָׁרֵשׁ	milczy	מַחֲשֶׁה
bieganie	מְרוּצָה	żywy (wieczny)	חַי, חָי
		zburzenie	חֻרְבָּן

1) **Zadanie**: Odmieniać rzeczowniki תְּחִנָּה־תְּחִנּוֹת, אֶרֶץ (אַרְצִי, אַרְצוֹתַי) w liczbie pojedynczej i mnogiej.

Lekcya LXXXII.

lekcya	לֶקַח, לְקָחִים	wyrywać, wykorzeniać, niszczyć	עָקַר
koperta	מַעֲטָפָה—פוֹת		

The year is 1967. I'm on vacation with my family in Niedzica. A woman who always asked questions of all sorts during meals tells me about my future, in which she envisions a husband, children, and a family. I'm twelve years old and I don't know yet the story of World War II nor the enormity of the death brought upon Polish and non-Polish Jews by the Holocaust, but I reply, "I'm never going to get married, because the one destined to be with me was never born. His would-be parents disappeared with the smoke from the crematorium furnaces." I clearly remember this conversation from so many years ago because I was horrified by my words as soon as I had uttered them. My memory is irrational, as it is tied to a world and people whom I could not possibly remember. It reaches back to an imagined, idealized world. This archive cannot be reorganized because the non-existent world that it documents also resists rearrangement. As do the deceased people who belonged to it, whom I have never met, and whose presence I feel nevertheless.

What tools are available to a person who cannot articulate her experiences because they persist in the realm of imagination and intuition more strongly than they do as real, tangible experiences? How do I live with the painful absence of non-existent yet close strangers, with an uncalled-for "archive" that is nevertheless installed in my memory, an archive that continually manifests itself in my emotions, my body, and my personal relationship with the space in which I live and work? What do I do with this archive when I lack the tools to transform this imagined catalogue into a real entity and free myself of it? Can I wrest myself away from this dybbuk? With no faith or outside support?

For as long as I can remember, I have lived with a sense of belonging to the world of central Europe, where Christians and Jews were together. The place inhabited by this other community—unknown, yet still present—is my imagination. As far back as my memory goes, I have missed them: the people who left before I even had the chance to meet them, and the people who were never born. For years this memory of a life that was not my own remained hidden within me, undisclosed to others, as if it were somehow shameful.

Despite numerous attempts and my desire to do so, I have never found in modern-day Poland or modern-day Israel anything that I could consider an extension of that world; nothing that would allow me to say goodbye and to close this painful part of my life. Perhaps only once during the several months I spent conducting research for the exhibition *Once We Were*, devoted to the topic of Tarnów Jews, did I have the feeling of "being close," if only for a few hours. I was having dinner with a group of young Israelis in Jaffa one evening. I felt as if we were in pre-World War II Warsaw. The houses surrounding us blurred together; we sat in silence as if thinking back to a time that we had all lost forever. Someone asked, "Where are you from?" "I'm from Poland," I replied. "You're not the only one," a young girl added. "We're all from Poland." That was the only time I have ever returned to that lost reality, to that world that will neither be replaced nor recreated by any museums.

As I walk the streets, lost in my thoughts, I keep imagining that it is my duty to preserve the memory of everyone I meet: people on photographs, portraits, and in films. I continually write the saddest of all dialogues: the one between different realities. And I lack the courage not to remember.

Ania Bujnowska and I spent over a year searching for archival photographs to be included in the exhibition *Once We Were* (Tarnów, 2014). We collected wonderful, touching images, and soon friends and strangers began coming to us with photographs, letters, and books that had been stored somewhere and then abandoned during the war. I would like to ponder each of these traces in silence; even the smallest among them contains its own story.

Kolomyja

Rabih Mroué

WARNING

The crocodile who ate the sun

How doth the little crocodile
Improve his shining tail,
And pour the waters of the Nile
On every golden scale!
How cheerfully he seems to grin,
How neatly spreads his claws,
And welcomes little fishes in
With gently smiling jaws!

(Lewis Carroll, *Alice's Adventures in Wonderland*, 1865)

I was 15 years old when the first Israeli leaflet fell from the sky and reached my hand. In July 1982, Beirut was under Israeli siege, and in one of those siege days the Israeli Air Forces dropped hundreds of thousands of leaflets into Beirut. A flock of pink flapping papers covered the sky and hid the burning sun. It was like snow in the middle of summer. The scene was incredible. As the papers fell from the sky, I jumped to catch one of them. There were few people in the streets then, some of them read the leaflet and laughed, others got angry. I witnessed three young fighters, two males and a female, tearing up the leaflets in a gesture of resistance, and while a woman in her forties looked up towards the sky cursing Israel, I started to read the leaflet. At that point in time, Israel was not only occupying the land and the sea but also our sky.

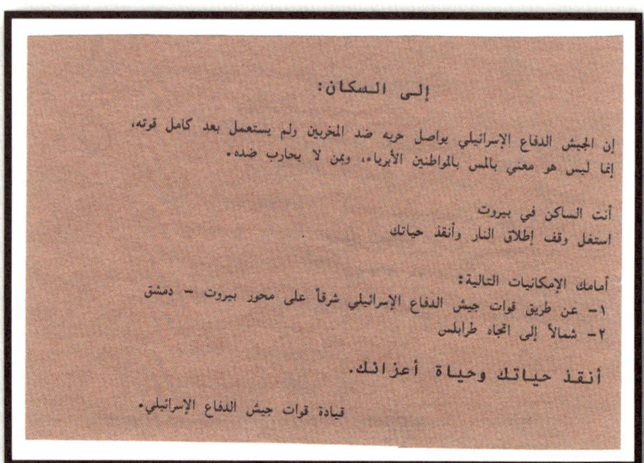
إلى السكان:

إن الجيش الدفاع الإسرائيلي يواصل حربه ضد المخربين ولم يستعمل بعد كامل قوته،
إنما ليس هو معني بالمس بالمواطنين الأبرياء، وبمن لا يحارب ضده.

أنت الساكن في بيروت
استغل وقف إطلاق النار وأنقذ حياتك

أمامك الإمكانيات التالية:
١- عن طريق قوات جيش الدفاع الإسرائيلي شرقاً على محور بيروت - دمشق
٢- شمالاً إلى اتجاه طرابلس

أنقذ حياتك وحياة أعزائك.

قيادة قوات جيش الدفاع الإسرائيلي.

To the residents:
The Israeli Defense Army continues its war against the vandals, and still has not used its full strength. However, the Army does not want to harm innocent citizens and those who do not fight against it.
To all those who live in Beirut:
take advantage of the cease-fire and save your life.

You have the following options:
1. Going through the Israeli Defense Forces point on the east axis of the Beirut-Damascus route.
2. Heading North, towards Tripoli.
Save your life and the life of your loved ones.

Command of the Israeli Defense Forces.

As I read the leaflet, I felt it was addressed to me personally. It was the first time that I got a written threat, but I was too young to realize that. I put it in my pocket and left indifferently. One hour later, the Israeli airplanes dropped their bombs over Beirut, and a black cloud engulfed the sky. The city was burning under the eclipsed sun.

I no longer recall where I put the leaflet; maybe I have lost it. I have searched for it in all the possible places, I asked everyone in the house about it, my mother, my father, my sister, and my brothers: the leaflet was not to be found anywhere. I was disappointed and felt sad as if I had lost a friend. Then, suddenly, I hit on the idea to make a replica of it.

Going back to that summer, a friend of mine disappeared with his two brothers between the two Beirut(s) while trying to get out of the besieged city from the east before heading towards the south of the country. It was their parents who insisted that the three brothers should leave West Beirut to a safe place. He has been missing ever since. I thought, there is always the possibility to make a replica of an object even if it's lost, but what to do when it comes to a missing friend?

Eventually, I managed to make a new leaflet that looked almost identical to the original one. Then I made some copies of it. For a while, I started to show it to visiting friends. None of them realized that this was a replica and I did not feel the need to mention the fact. They all believed that it was actually the original leaflet. The way these replicas evoked their memories from that period was magical. Everyone started telling me about that summer of Beirut '82. They told me about their experiences, and shared some of their personal and intimate stories. Some of them were really sad, others were so funny and cheerful. While talking, most of them would hold the leaflets between their hands, unconsciously playing with the pieces of paper and handling them in different manners; mostly they ended up damaging them. When they were done, they would realize what they had done to the leaflet, then they would apologize with a little smile and would leave, keeping the leaflets on the table in their new conditions.

I used to collect these leaflets, photograph them and write the stories that my friends told me while crumpling them, folding them, or writing all over them… I intended to use them for a theatre piece, but then I dropped the idea for reasons I have forgotten now.

In fact, in the same way that I have lost the original leaflet, I also lost the replicas and the stories I wrote. This time, though, I was neither disappointed nor sad. Out of all these materials, only the photographs of the "damaged" leaflets survived, as well as the memory of "The crocodile who ate the sun," a story one of my friends told me.

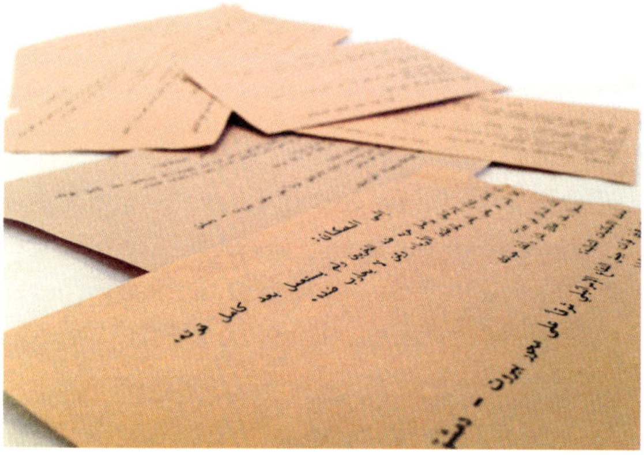

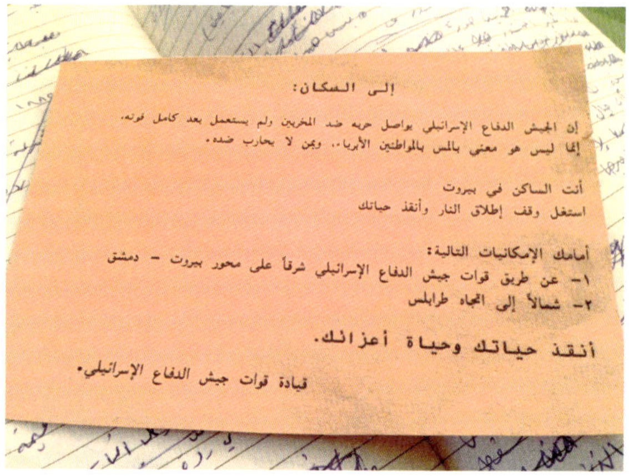

Thinking about it now, I wonder whether my desire was to archive the original leaflet or to document what happened to the replicas I made? Whether my attempt was to recall the people's reactions at the moment they received the warning leaflet in 1982 or to record the symptomatic traces my friends left on my replicas?

Anyway, I remember that I wanted to make a kind of statistical comparison between the numbers of Israeli leaflets dropped over Beirut in summer '82 and the number of the besieged people at that time, in order to calculate how many people must have received the leaflets, estimate the number of those who had torn them up, how many had kept them after reading it and the ones who had just thrown them away and gone. Maybe it was a belief that the numerical relations gained by assembling phenomena and facts and by connecting them can enable us to understand our present or predict our future.

When I look at these photographs now, I see fake documents holding inside some sincere moments. I can also feel the passing of time and the nostalgia for that place. I hardly remember the dates, the names, my friends' faces, and my little secrets. In between the original and the copy, Beirut was an "original" city in 1982; luckily, we lost it in the midst of the darkness and nothing is left for us now but a copy of a copy of a copy: beautiful copies of forgotten memories. What is certain is that the darkness in Beirut has nothing to do with the crocodile who ate the sun and became proud of its lit-up and shining belly. Not at all. Beirut's blackout came mainly from the same chronic power cuts that are still hitting the whole country at the time of writing this text.

Most probably, the photographs of the leaflet replicas are nothing but a playful way of dealing with a history full of tragedies and sorrows, or maybe they are like a fast-food meal to chew upon at a time of a desertification of minds. They might also help us recall a small incident to tickle the memory of our absentee history.

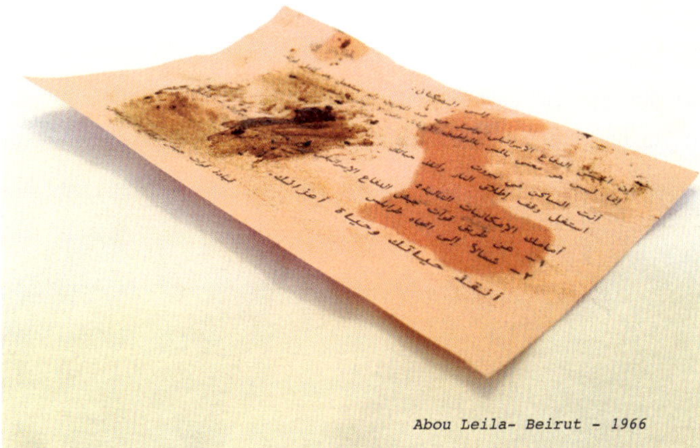

Abou Leila- Beirut - 1966

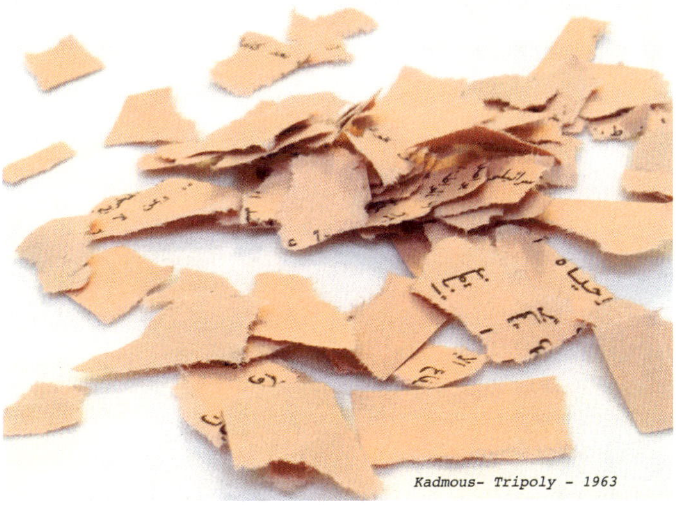

Kadmous- Tripoly - 1963

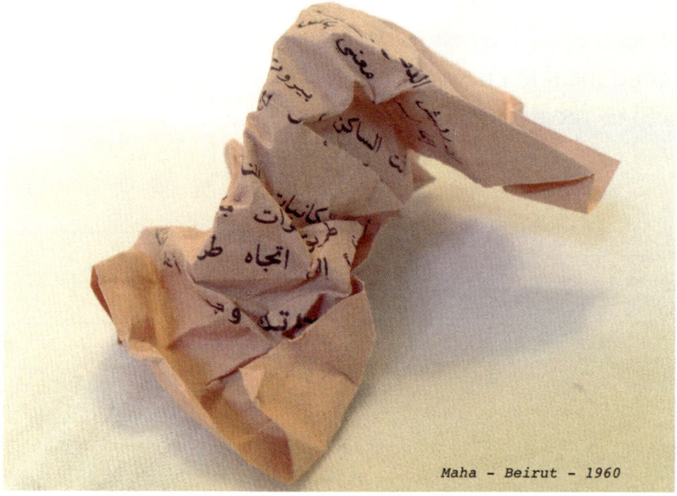

Maha - Beirut - 1960

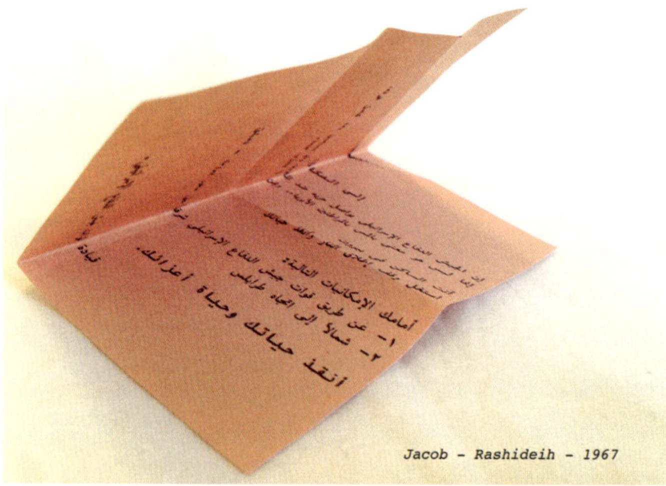

Jacob - Rashideih - 1967

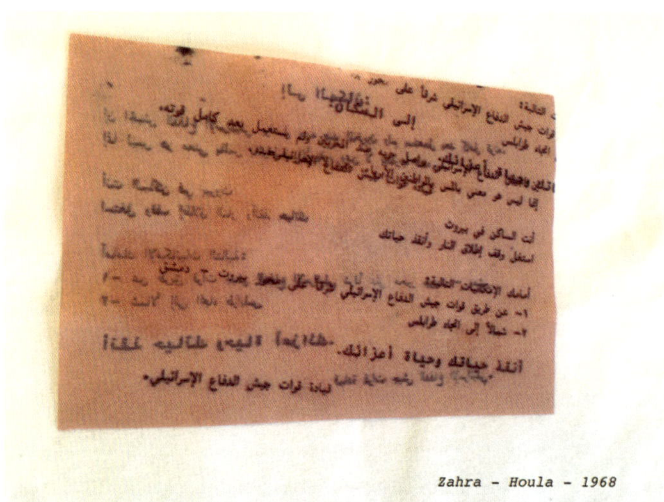

Zahra - Houla - 1968

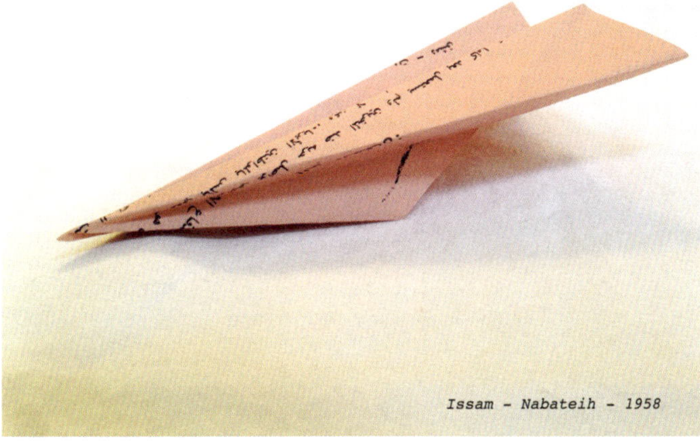

Issam - Nabateih - 1958

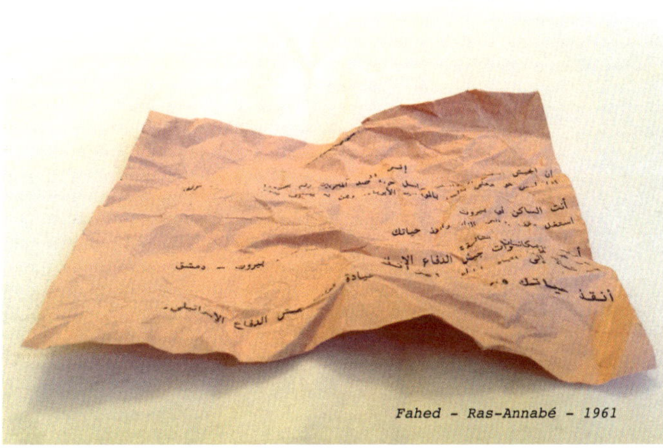

Fahed - Ras-Annabé - 1961

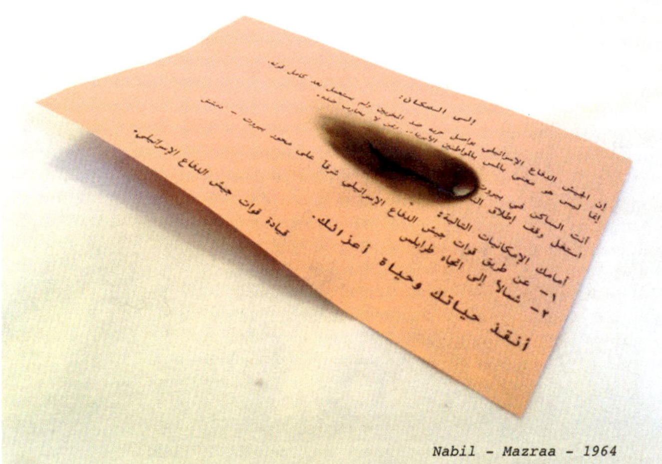

Nabil - Mazraa - 1964

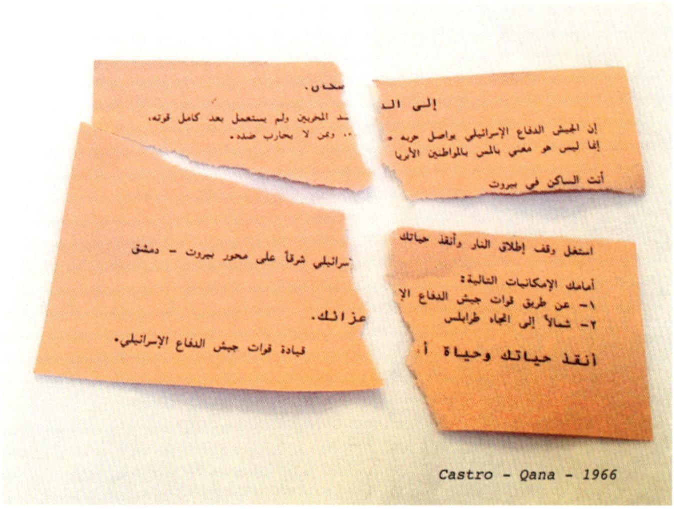

Castro - Qana - 1966

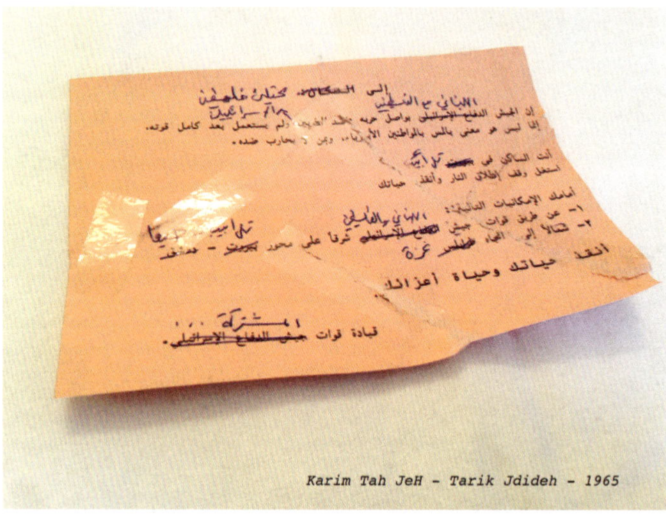

Karim Tah JeH - Tarik Jdideh - 1965

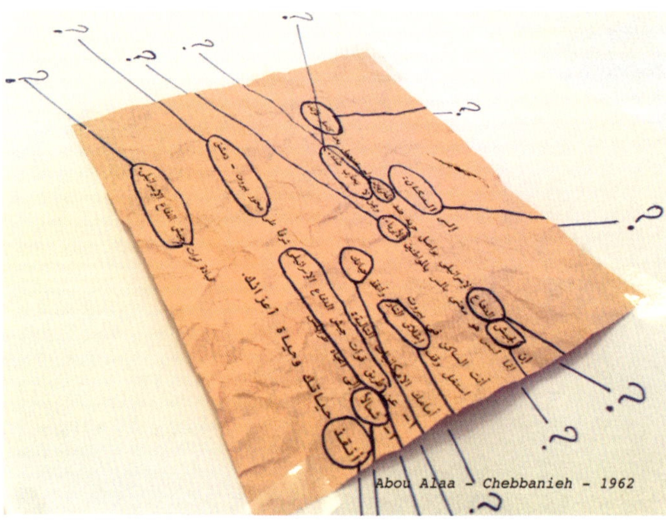

Abou Alaa - Chebbanieh - 1962

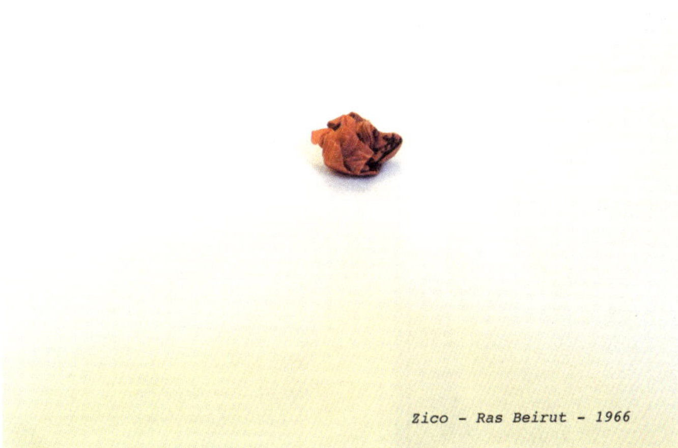

Appendix

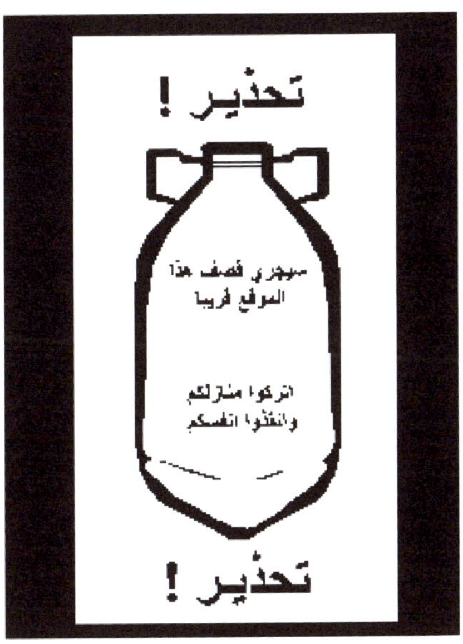

Warning!

This location will soon be bombed.
Leave your houses and save your life.

Warning!

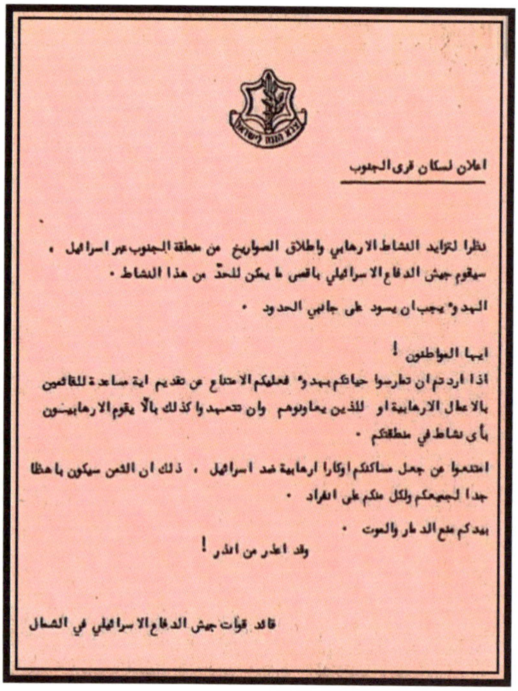

اعلان لسكان قرى الجنوب

نظرا لتزايد النشاط الارهابي واطلاق الصواريخ من منطقة الجنوب عبر اسرائيل ،
سيقوم جيش الدفاع الاسرائيلي باقصى ما يمكن للحدّ من هذا النشاط .
الهدوء يجب ان يسود على جانبي الحدود .

ايها المواطنون !
اذا اردتم ان تمارسوا حياتكم بهدوء فعليكم الامتناع عن تقديم اية مساعدة للقائمين بالاعمال الارهابية او للذين يعاونوهم وان تتعهدوا كذلك بالّا يقوم الارهابيون بأي نشاط في منطقتكم .

امتنعوا من جعل مساكنكم اوكارا ارهابية ضد اسرائيل ، ذلك ان الثمن سيكون باهظا جدا لجميعكم ولكل منكم على انفراد .
بيدكم منع الدمار والموت .
وقد اعذر من انذر !

قائد قوات جيش الدفاع الاسرائيلي في الشمال

<u>*Announcement to the inhabitants of the southern villages*</u>

Due to the increase in terrorist activity and the launching of missiles from the South into Israel, the Israeli Defense Forces will act to curtail these activities.
Calm must prevail on both sides of the border.
Citizens!
If you want to pursue your day-to-day life in peace, you must cease providing assistance to those engaging in terrorist acts or those helping them. You should also take it upon yourself to ensure that no terrorist activity takes place in your area.
Don't allow your homes to become terrorist dens against Israel, or the price will be very costly for all of you, both collectively and individually.
It is in your hands to stop destruction and death.
Ignorance is no excuse for those who have been forewarned.

The Commander of the Northern Israeli Defense Forces

Israel leaflet dropped over the south of Lebanon in 1981.

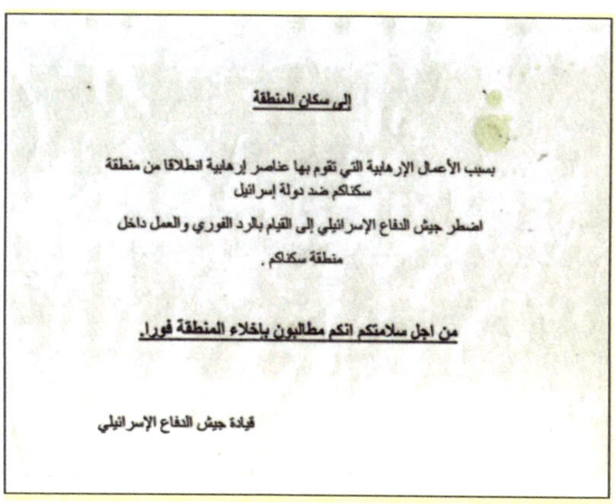

إلى سكان المنطقة

بسبب الأعمال الإرهابية التي تقوم بها عناصر إرهابية انطلاقا من منطقة سكناكم ضد دولة إسرائيل
اضطر جيش الدفاع الإسرائيلي إلى القيام بالرد الفوري والعمل داخل منطقة سكناكم .

من اجل سلامتكم انكم مطالبون بإخلاء المنطقة فورا.

قيادة جيش الدفاع الإسرائيلي

<u>To the residents of the neighbourhood</u>

<u>Read this statement carefully and follow its instructions.</u>

Heinous terrorist acts have emanated from your neighbourhood, exemplified by firing rockets towards the State of Israel. Starting from this moment, the Israeli Defense Forces will act with all its strength against the terrorist gang.
For your safety!
You are ordered to evacuate the area immediately by heading northwards.
Whoever remains in the area will put his life at risk.

The State of Israel

Israel leaflet dropped over Gaza in January 2009.

Claudia Castellucci

ORDIGNO

DEVICE

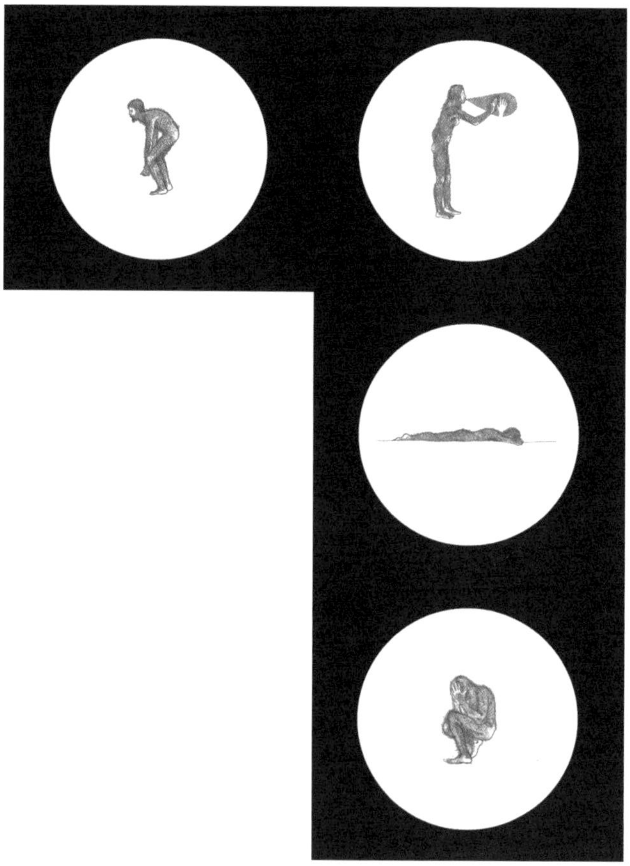

Instructions:

for the Historic Device. It is a handbook of gestures assembled in the form of a book with eight sides opening out like a concertina. One places it before herself, opens it, and starts imitating the depicted gestures for a sufficient time, shifting from one position to the next with fluid gestures and a regular rhythm. At the end, one closes the Device and sets it down.

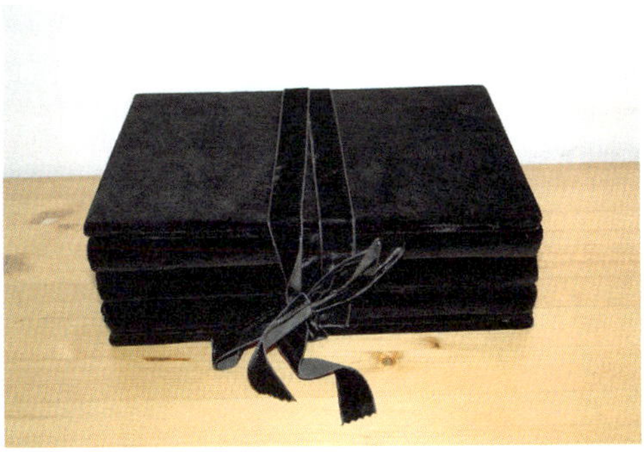

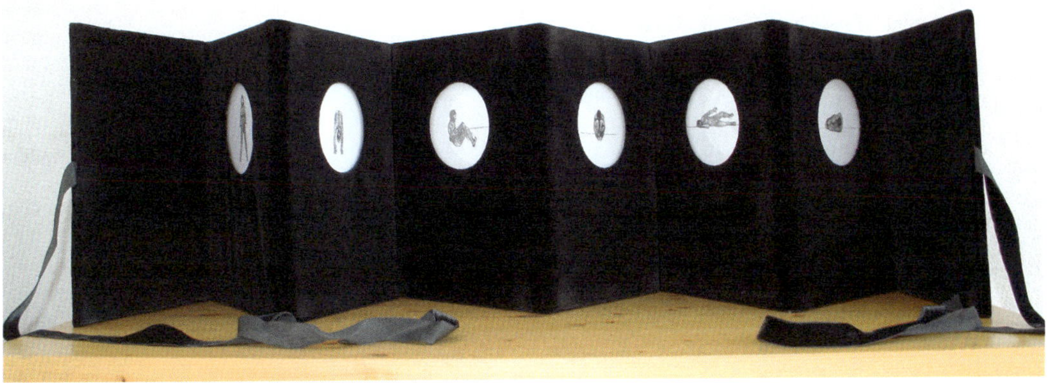

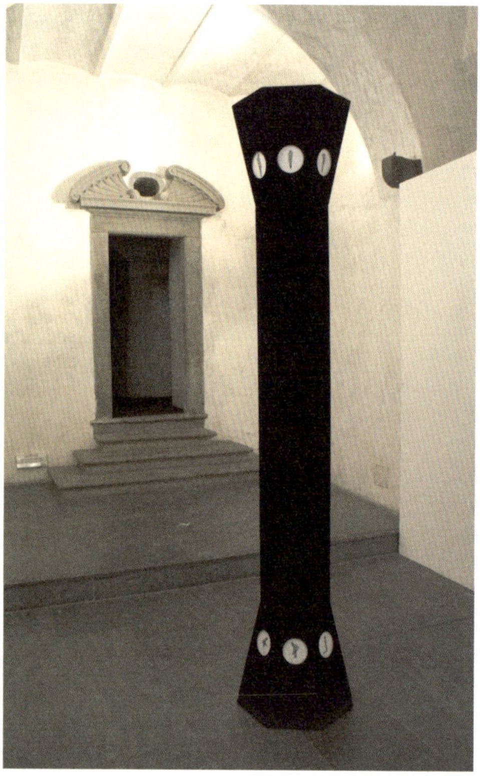

Instructions:

for the Historic Column. Seven people take their position around the column, each facing one of the seven sides of its plinth, imitating the gesture depicted there. After a sufficient pause, one says softly: "Let us proceed." All move to the next position, according to a principle of fluid transformation, ready to apprehend and embody the new gesture. The motion will be to the right if in the Southern Hemisphere, to the left if in the Northern. The rotation will be complete once the seventh side of the base has been reached. Subsequently, the seven sides of the capital are engaged with one at a time in the same manner. At the end, one signals the completion of the cycle by saying softly: "The end." All disperse.

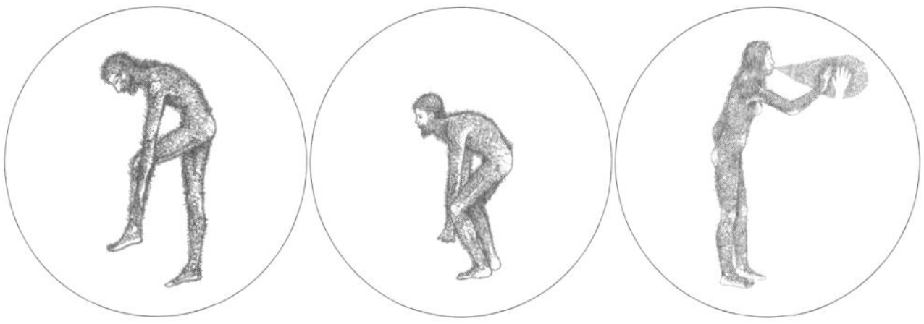

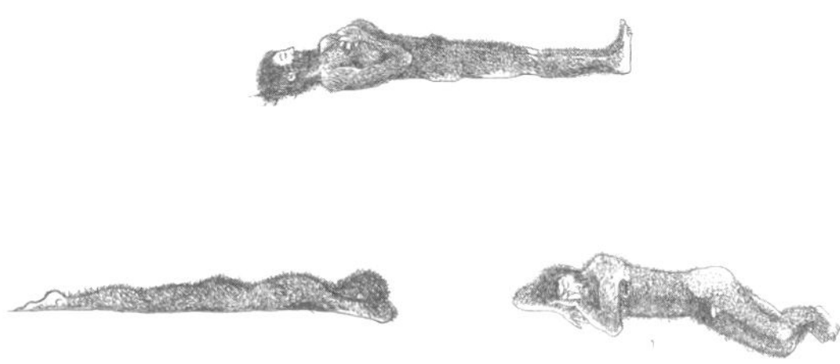

A device is an object that imagines and prepares a future event. Like a trap. It is also an ornamental object treating the past as something that can always be brought back into circulation and re-actualized. Tools, handbooks, and monuments are all works that have a timely concreteness: the kind of art that deploys them in our day is worthy of the name of craft. It is an art that nurtures something that is inherently real.

Franz Anton Cramer

BEWEGUNG

MOVEMENT

Collecting defies time, insofar as time is equated with decay. Collecting is meant to preserve, but it can only take place in time. It is a movement through time, and in time, a collection becomes an archive. A collection represents the time from which its holdings have broken free without being able to escape completely. Mario Wimmer writes in his study on "archival bodies" called *Archivkörper* that an archive is "like an organism consisting of a bureaucratic rationality and the history kept alive within it." Archives are "places where time is embodied." In his investigation of spectacular cases of archival materials stolen from German and Austrian collections in the interwar years, Wimmer comes to the conclusion that it was all "about the relationship between science and passion."

Movement does not happen only at the beginning of an archive; document theft is also a form of movement. Movement could thus be regarded as a part of the life of an archive. The movement from one place to another not only characterizes the collection itself; it is also necessary for getting to, or entering the archive, as well as leaving it.

The International Dance Archive (Archives Internationales de la Danse, A.I.D.) was an institution that existed in Paris between 1931 and 1952. Its activities included organizing exhibitions, collecting data, archiving historical reproductions, and publishing a magazine devoted to dance. It also organized, supervised, and financed choreography competitions (the most well-known featured the premiere of Kurt Jooss' ballet *The Green Table* in 1932). Finally, it organized research trips overseas, and collected, researched, and introduced French and European folk dance as a scholarly field.

The leading figure behind the development and monitoring of all these activities was Pierre Tugal. Tugal had been born as Ilya Micheleff Epschtein in 1883 in Tauragē, which was at that time under Russian administration and is now part of Latvia. Tugal earned a Ph.D. in law and had been living in France since 1913. He had studied in Germany, Switzerland, and Belgium and had become interested in dance through journalism. Tugal wanted to liberate the academic study of dance from anecdotal evidence and base it on the scientific methods already available for the study of history, philology, art history, and anthropology. Ultimately, his goal was to centre the archive on movement.

I was one of several scholars who participated in a four-year research project investigating the A.I.D.'s archival holdings, its intellectual vision, its treatment of movement, and its influence on the political situation of artist émigrés from Germany in the 1930s. In addition, we researched the whereabouts of the archive's documents after World War II and after the archive closed for good in 1952. The project was also concerned with trying to understand and reconstruct Tugal's life, because hidden behind the collected books, photographs, essays, films, and memorandums was a figure that continually evaded our grasp.

All this changed overnight when the nieces of Tugal's brother-in-law (his sister Thérèse had been married to the Polish composer Alexandre Tansman) handed the research team an inconspicuous briefcase. This turned out to contain Pierre Tugal's only remaining personal documents in a mouldy and creased state. The papers had reached the two women in a roundabout way after his death, and they were glad to finally entrust them to someone.

The last years of Tugal's life (he died in 1964) were marked by poverty and isolation. After the archive's dissolution, against which Tugal never stopped fighting, he worked tirelessly to prevent the collection from being scattered. He was unsuccessful, however, as our research showed, time and again. We frequently found documents with the A.I.D. stamp at flea markets, in other libraries, at Internet auctions, and even in the hands of dubious art dealers.

The briefcase contained numerous drafts for articles and books with which Tugal had undoubtedly hoped to kindle the waning interest in dance as a scholarly practice. Whilst these books were never written, the drafts are now available on the website of the Centre National de la Danse near Paris, meaning they are now part of another archive.

It seems to be the fate of archives that they must follow the movement of their founders' lives in time—including the movement towards oblivion. By following this movement and reconstructing it, we can comprehend and retrace the permanent link between the act of collecting and the personal history of people and their collections. In this way, we can reconstruct the historically specific, as well as existential, task that marks the beginning of each collection.

The life story of Pierre Tugal, an émigré whose application for French citizenship was repeatedly turned down, can now be described fairly well, even if we are primarily limited to the history of its events. This is more than many of the refugees now arriving in western Europe can claim. Their identity cards are often destroyed by the same human traffickers who organize their movement. It is the task of the refugees—and sometimes my own (as an aid and interpreter)—to reconstruct their life stories and to support this with evidence against a backdrop that could hardly be more urgent. On their journey across borders, cultures, and identities, their archive is lost. It is sacrificed in the name of movement.

The movement of refugees through identities, political systems, and countries increases their dependency on systems of belief. Incidentally, this is also a fundamental principle of every archive. A birth certificate is more important than an actual birth. Identity is not provided by existence; it is provided by a document. In German administrative law, there is even something called a "life certificate" (*Lebensbescheinigung*, or "certificat de vie") that officially proves that a person is not dead.

Neither Tugal's life nor his identity was ever in question. Yet, he never remained the same person. His draft for an essay on the objective criticism of dance is presumably the last legacy of a person who had pursued the archive as much as he had watched over it. Movement never stops, life does. Decades later, the actual task of any archive of movement was finally revealed by the loss of Tugal's life-time work: never remain in the archive—in other words, never value the traces of life more than life itself.

Elisabeth Lebovici

SIDA

AIDS

In 2013, I was asked to participate in the first conference to be devoted to Lionel Soukaz, a gay experimental filmmaker born in 1953. The academic celebration was also organized to mark the "material" recognition of Soukaz's work undertaken by the Archives françaises du film (French Film Archives) concerning the restoration of the film strips, and by the Bibliothèque Nationale de France (National Library of France) for the digitization of the videos. Indeed, his films, emblematic of the movements of sexual and artistic dissidence of the 1970s (and in particular of the Front Homosexuel d'Action Révolutionnaire, or FHAR, the Homosexual Front of Revolutionary Action, with its charismatic thinker Guy Hocquenghem), were rediscovered only at the beginning of the 2000s. Often censored, Lionel Soukaz's films in the 1980s took on the task to show what was happening to the "community of fags, poor people, and drug users" decimated by AIDS but also mobilized in the struggle. The epidemic also got the better of Lionel Soukaz's films: he stopped producing them in 1986, turning his "desperate vitality" to other forms of experimentation, in particular video and digital work.

So it came about that, spending several days in the audio-visual room at National Library in Paris, I was able to watch some of the over 2000 hours composing the artist's video journal, begun in 1991 and providing the exclusive focus for his activity over the course of the following decade. The public institution's audio-visual archive had received the artist's consent concerning the conservation and digitization of this form of memory.

I emerged from this full immersion in a daze. From one filmed sequence and video tape to the next, these rushes give an all-round picture of the deadliest decade of gay and lesbian life in France—a perspective that never neglects the radical ways in which film can embody its subject.

"In April 1991, I start a journal: *Annals* [...] On May 6th, 1991, I film the demonstration of LGBT groups against the draft legislation debated in the French Senate," one can find written on YouTube and Daily Motion, two networks where Lionel Soukaz (under his pseudonym LeSouk) has left a number of his videos for anyone to watch.

These are full immersion videos: the camera is carried on the body and films the experience from inside, merging with the group of demonstrators, with the bodies, faces, and gestures among which it finds itself, without ever distancing itself far enough to take stock. In those years, the frame was literally invaded by AIDS, by the struggle against AIDS that arose, as we used to say in Act Up-Paris, "from the gay community" (and from that of intravenous drug users, who Soukaz never forgets). Thus, the writing of self that Lionel Soukaz performed in 1991 combines two elements: the image (the "filmage", i.e. the image in action) and AIDS. The two elements are "at battle" for life and until death, at the same time. Filming is a vital action while bodies are disappearing. As Simon Watney observed, as early as 1987: "AIDS is not only a medical crisis of unprecedented depth. It implies a crisis of representation itself. A crisis that affects all we know about the human body and its capacities for sexual pleasure." One, moreover, that cannot but overwhelm the "I" that writes or represents.

Lionel Soukaz filmed many forms of speech: the slogans at demonstrations and the chats among friends using the "camp slang" that has been analysed by many commentators; incredibly intimate monologues from friends and lovers, as well as innumerable sessions of seminars, courses, assemblies, film presentations, conferences… Not to mention the remarkable presence of words coming from the TV. Soukaz watched TV and recorded the images and TV shows through which, starting in 1993, the representations of AIDS were being channelled , thus providing a history of AIDS on TV, a history of the change in AIDS representation on TV, as well as a history of the evolution of TV and its genres.

The degree of Soukaz's appropriation of televised images is revealed in the confrontation it stages by almost systematically showing someone *watching* TV, often talking back to it in passing. At the heart of this confrontation we find RV (acronym for Hervé, his lover), or rather RV in bed and at RV's bedside, the rage of the person with AIDS. AIDS is a war against TV. Lionel Soukaz shows the degree to which TV is the place where the notions of public and private get blurred. State, or "public" TV—including the commercial or "private" networks—has been watched in homes since the 1960s, and has often focused on the privacy of some leading character publicly exposed in the media, particularly when that person "comes out" as having AIDS.

One could say that by watching TV and recording it, Lionel Soukaz has produced an incomparable form of televisual archive, on the one hand sexually "oriented", while on the other coupled with recordings of images from the daily life of his sick lover, of the friend pointing out the run-down medical institution where he was hospitalized. A counter-television is born. The body is so deeply invested in the form and rhythm of the image, which breathes like a lung, that we might call this activity "Actionism". Lionel Soukaz unearths one of the crucial characteristics of TV: that it feeds on its own images, constantly recontextualizing them into its own flux.

The second corpus of images in the *Annals* refers to the demonstrations that Lionel filmed while attending them, both as a participant and an activist. This is why the recordings are so long, sometimes taking up more than one 90-minute tape. It is out of the question to separate, as the media normally do, the "die-in" from a December 1st march or a "Day of Desperation", or to film just the people at the head of a Gay Pride parade and the political personalities who are usually there barely long enough for an interview, or to show just the highlights of a weekly Act-Up-Paris meeting in 1993 and 1994.

Embedded within the demonstrations, one also finds archived many elements that hail from the field of visual arts: artists' "filmage"; filmed exhibitions; films showing the mounting of exhibitions. Snatches of recorded conferences. Meetings. The visual register is associated with a name: Michel Journiac, the emblematic artist of "body art" in France, himself associated with radical movements and particularly with FHAR. Journiac was one of the charismatic teachers at the University of Visual Arts at Paris 1, where he directed a research centre on "The stakes of representation: the body."

For both Journiac and Soukaz, the body is the active agent that calls the finality of art into question, exceeding the traditional aesthetic field and its representations to situate itself "as a body questioning the political, social, and sexual" (Journiac). Naturally, AIDS was at the centre of Journiac's work and of the exhibitions he organized with his students and former students right up to his death in 1995. In filming these exhibitions and the activist interventions in introductory seminars with the students, Soukaz resurrects a nearly forgotten memory, one that belies the commonplace that "in France, the art world has done nothing against AIDS." The recordings are there to prove the contrary.

They have also persuaded me that we need to change our point of view as to what we call "the art world." If one merely follows the logic of cultural recognition accorded to canonical aesthetic practices, and thinks of art as an autonomous institution without any social function, then the visibility of AIDS is probably not so obvious. One should accordingly shift the attention towards artists and practices, most of the time collective, that have focused, precisely, on "The stakes of representation: the body."

Lionel Soukaz's *Annals* have thus provided an alternative archive from which I can produce a memory—one that goes far beyond my own—of what AIDS "did" in the field of representation. Yet, this *filmage sauvage* still remains more or less inaccessible, and will for long remain so, both for copyright reasons (Soukaz never asked for permission to film) and for lack of time. Who, today, has thousands of hours to spare in order to watch the archive in its entirety? To whom, then, are these *Annals* addressed? I would suggest they are addressed to researchers, whether they are dealing with history, social struggle, homosexuality, activism, television, art, or archives. It is this counter-public, this community of researchers, spanning a broad range of interests, who is just waiting to take shape and form a body.

Bettina Knaup

RECOMBINATIONS

In recent years, I have been more or less intensively involved in the construction, maintenance, and circulation of a growing temporary collection of feminist performance documents. We, the curator Beatrice E. Stammer and I, called this project a "performing archive". We were thus using the idea of the archive in a broader sense—rather as an aspiration in the sense of Arjun Appadurai, or as a suggestion for an archive in the process of becoming. In actuality, it was a temporary collection of videos, films, and photographs on loan from roughly 180 feminist and queer performance artists from around the globe. It travelled throughout Europe for more than two years, during which it was supplemented, extended, and modified. In the end, the collection was dissolved.

When the editors of this volume asked me to consider what moved, excited, and emotionally touched me most in my numerous "archival encounters" with feminist (performance) history during those years, I can say it was those moments when singular objects of historiography (a performance document, a video, a photograph) began to merge with diverse networks of relations, with embodied everyday practices, and dissolve into movement, thus enabling encounters across space and time. In her study *Why Stories Matter*, Clare Hemmings described such a space of possibility for (feminist) encounters, in which she explored how feminist history and stories could be written and told differently, in a transformative way, thus making it possible "to grasp the possibility of feminist spaces of friendship, desire, affiliation, and productivity that produce variegated historical accounts, whose subject (of any age) *shuttle back and forth* between their own and other's memories, representations, and fantasies of past, present and future."

Oddly enough, I think of two performances that at first do not seem to have much, if anything, to do with archival practices but seem more related to the domestic world. Nonetheless, they symbolize for me the use of an archive as an embodied space of becoming and of encounters, where participants can inhabit stories and move back and forth between them.

Una cosa es una cosa is a performance by the artist María Teresa Hincapié. She performed it four times in Colombia and Venezuela in 1990, each time for 18 days, 12 hours each day. The Brazilian artist and author Eleonora Fabião contributed this performance story to the *re.act.feminism* archive.

In a large room, numerous bags and boxes containing countless objects from the artist's private household are lying in the middle of the floor. She unpacks each item, one after the other, spreading them out and organizing them: clothes, rolled up and placed in a line of pink, black, white, and red; the line continues around the corner at a right angle from the outside, forming an inward square spiral; the clothes are followed by larger sacks and cloth bags, underwear, nylon stockings, used paper bags, plastic bowls, packages of lentils and beans, shoes, a small wooden board, used small white paper bags, used large brown paper bags, root vegetables, an electric water boiler, a box, plates of various shapes and sizes, potatoes (again and again), cutlery, a powder compact, a feather, a rubber band, jewellery, potatoes next to the jewellery, more food stuffs, orange rubber gloves, a pot with a blue lid, an orange plastic strainer, a brown paper gift bag, withered spring onions, lined up cowry shells, white candles, a reusable lid for bottles, paper tissues, potatoes, onions, lipsticks, toothbrush, three cosmetic jars, paper clips arranged in a long row, hair curlers, matches in a line, a matchbox, pins stuck in the floor. The line goes on and on, right angle after right angle. Then the objects are sorted again and rearranged, the rows are interrupted, the clear form of the square spiral is disturbed, and clothes are unfolded, spreading the emptiness caused by their abandonment. The lines acquire more form and depth, new proximities are formed; then, the things are collected, little piles are generated, things are stacked, shifted, packed in boxes, filled in little paper bags, and tidied away.

I only see a small part of it. It goes on for hours, days. She brings her own mattress and sometimes sleeps, lying down among the objects. After a while, stories of used, everyday, simple, unglamorous, and found objects evolve—objects connected to bodies, objects that clothe, feed, nurture, and adorn; objects that store, connect, or close up; objects that convey memories, but also ones that decay or are seen as waste. They refer to the repetitive work of the household, office, and factory, to poverty, to migration. They are kept, collected, taken along, reused, recombined, reassessed, touched lovingly, rearranged, packaged, stored, unpacked, and disposed of. They are witnesses of use and of touch; they prompt us to feel them, to pick them up, to carry them back and forth, to touch them, to set them down, to observe them, to use them. They form endless lines, spirals, connections.

The other performance is *Domestic Sanitation* by Helen Chadwick. This performance was part of Chadwick's final thesis at the Academy of Art in Brighton in 1976. The grainy Super 8 footage shows four women in surreal latex, hair, and bondage costumes in a room that oscillates between a beauty salon, a doctor's surgery, and a fitness gym. They try out different mysterious devices—body massage bands, large brushes, stretch bands, poles, foils, portable massage tables, and a piece of latex cloth stretched vertically on a wooden frame.

They prance, strut, relax, rock back and forth, comb each other's merkins, or they brush, massage, and treat each other. They stretch their muscles, they loll and slouch. Sometimes the camera comes closer, and the latex, skin folds, hair, powder, and foils merge into an abstract landscape of pixels. It seems as though these latex-clad beings appropriate this conglomeration of tools of female domestic subjugation only to turn them into their own objects of play and pleasure. In the next scene, "bed women" appear—a swinging-bed woman, a pink boudoir woman with a white pillow wig and a dress made of sheets, an unruly housewife, and a mattress woman dancing ecstatically. The objects, the silent inventory comes to life. It does not completely leave behind its history of oppression, but extends and stretches it, thus somehow derailing it.

I dream of an archive that we could inhabit for a while, together or alone. Where we could exchange, share, touch, re-perform, and recombine objects, stories, and documents for several hours or days, or at least once in a while. Where we could bring things. Where we could sleep, sit, lie down, walk, dance, play, meditate, talk, or misbehave. Where the everyday, the discarded, the traumatic, and the pleasurable all have a place. Where the process of archiving becomes "maintenance art", in the sense of Mierle Laderman Ukeles, who in her 1969 *Manifesto for Maintenance Art* declared the everyday work of caring, maintaining, repairing, and recombining to be art. In other words, I dream of archiving as an embodied, devoted, and everyday practice that is not removed from the rest of our lives, and that preserves, nurtures, and promotes our multifaceted relations to (his and her)stories of resistance.

Erik Göngrich

EINMACHGLAS

PRESERVE JAR

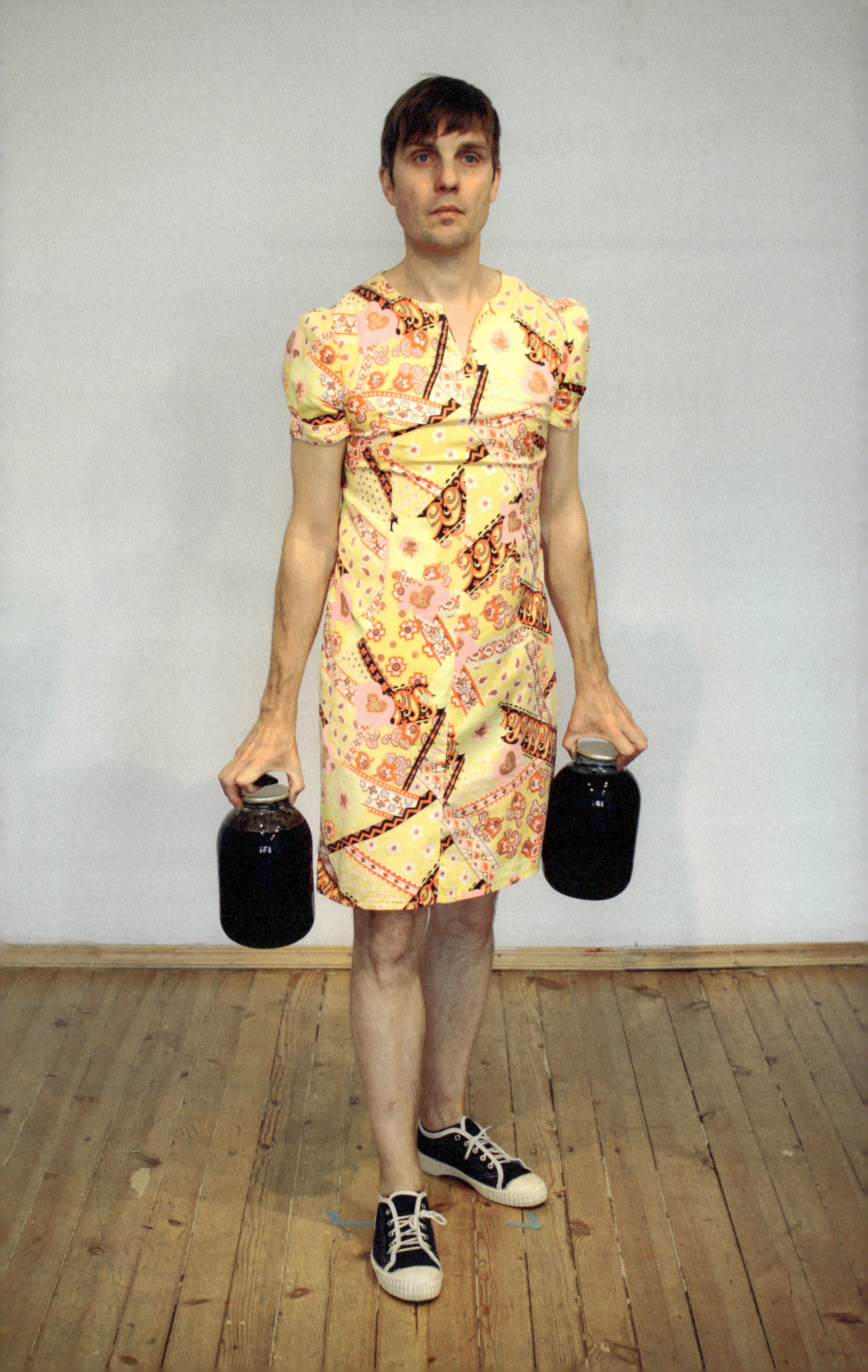

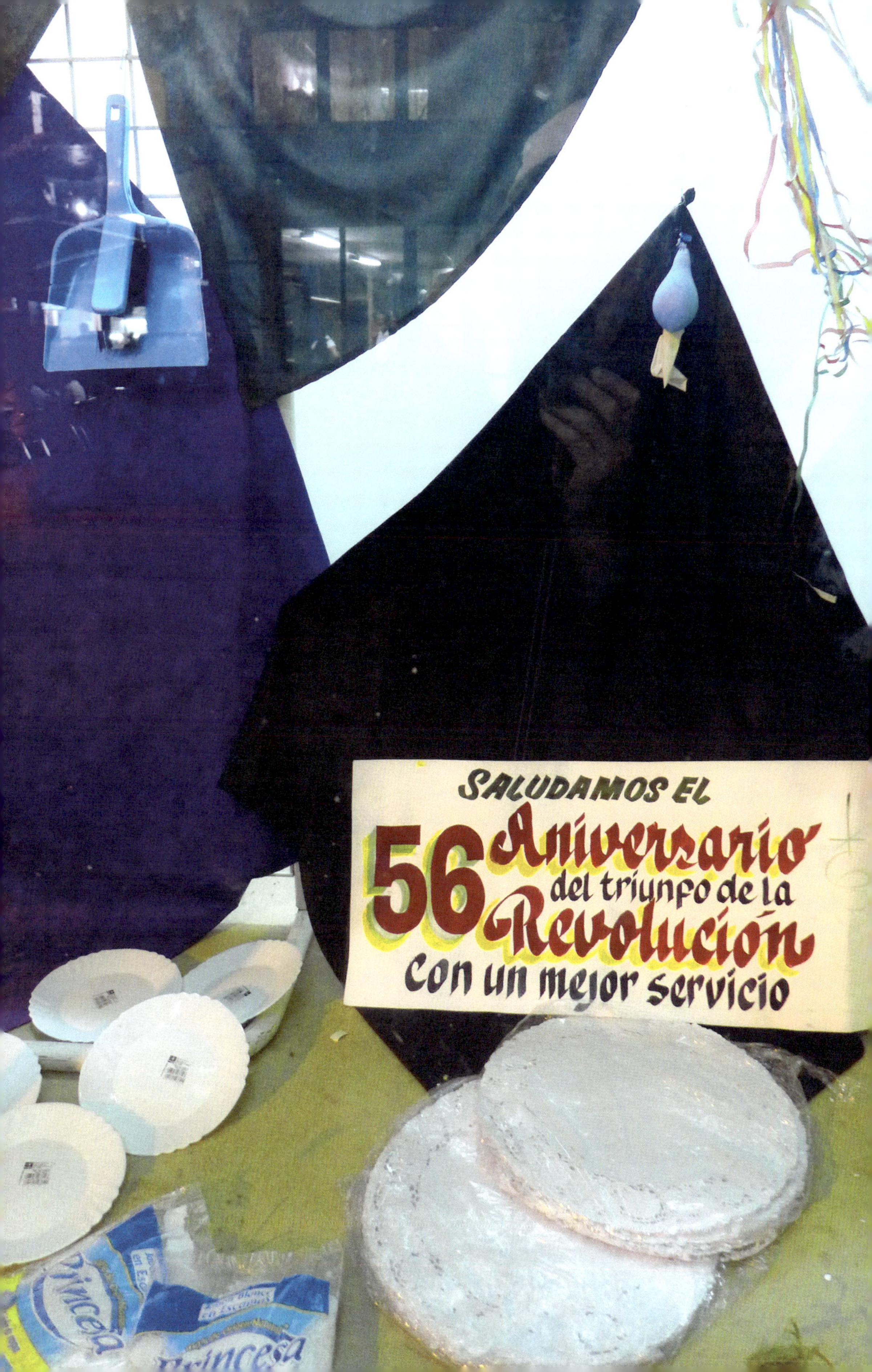
SALUDAMOS EL
56 Aniversario
del triunfo de la
Revolución
con un mejor servicio

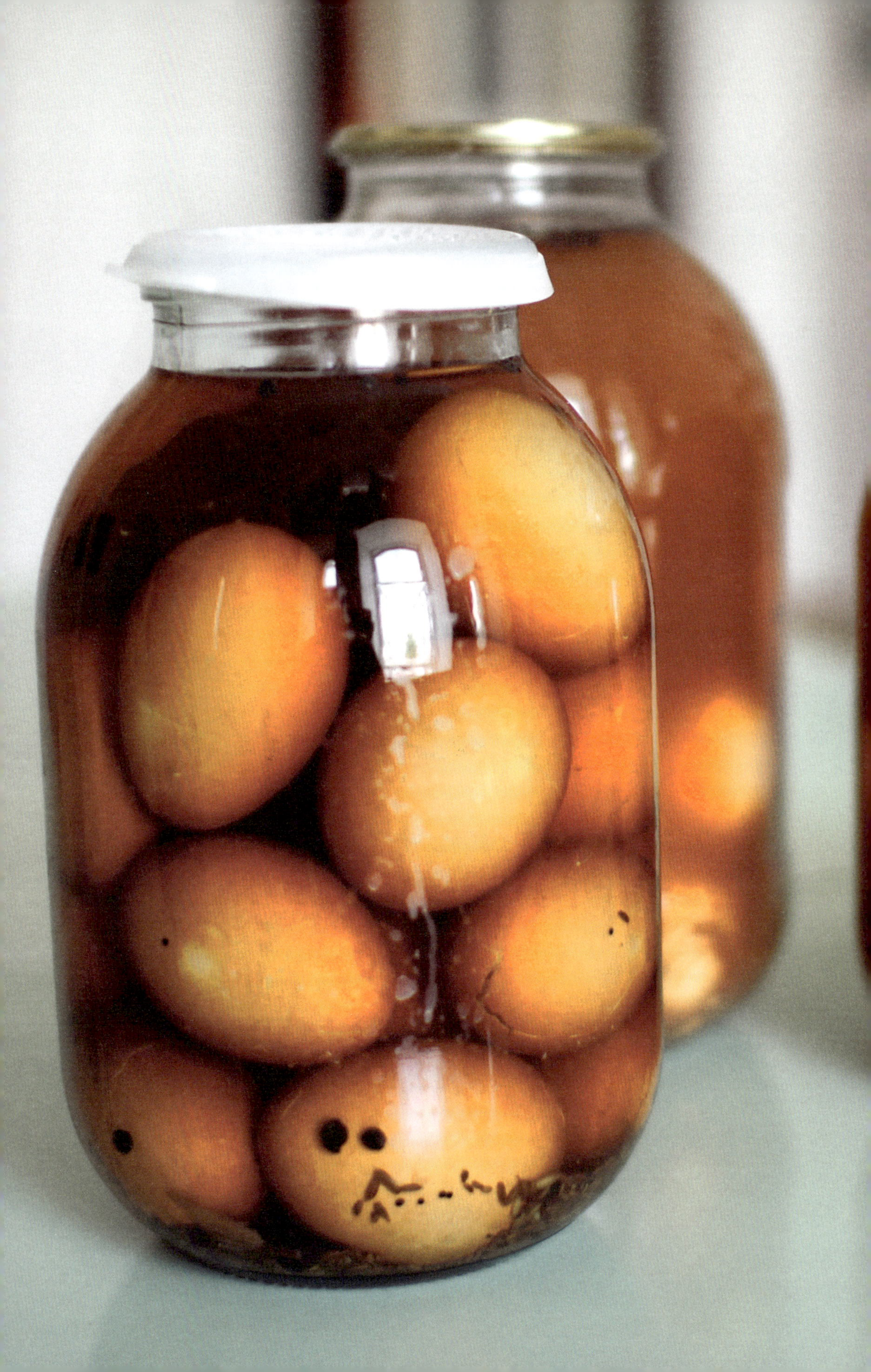

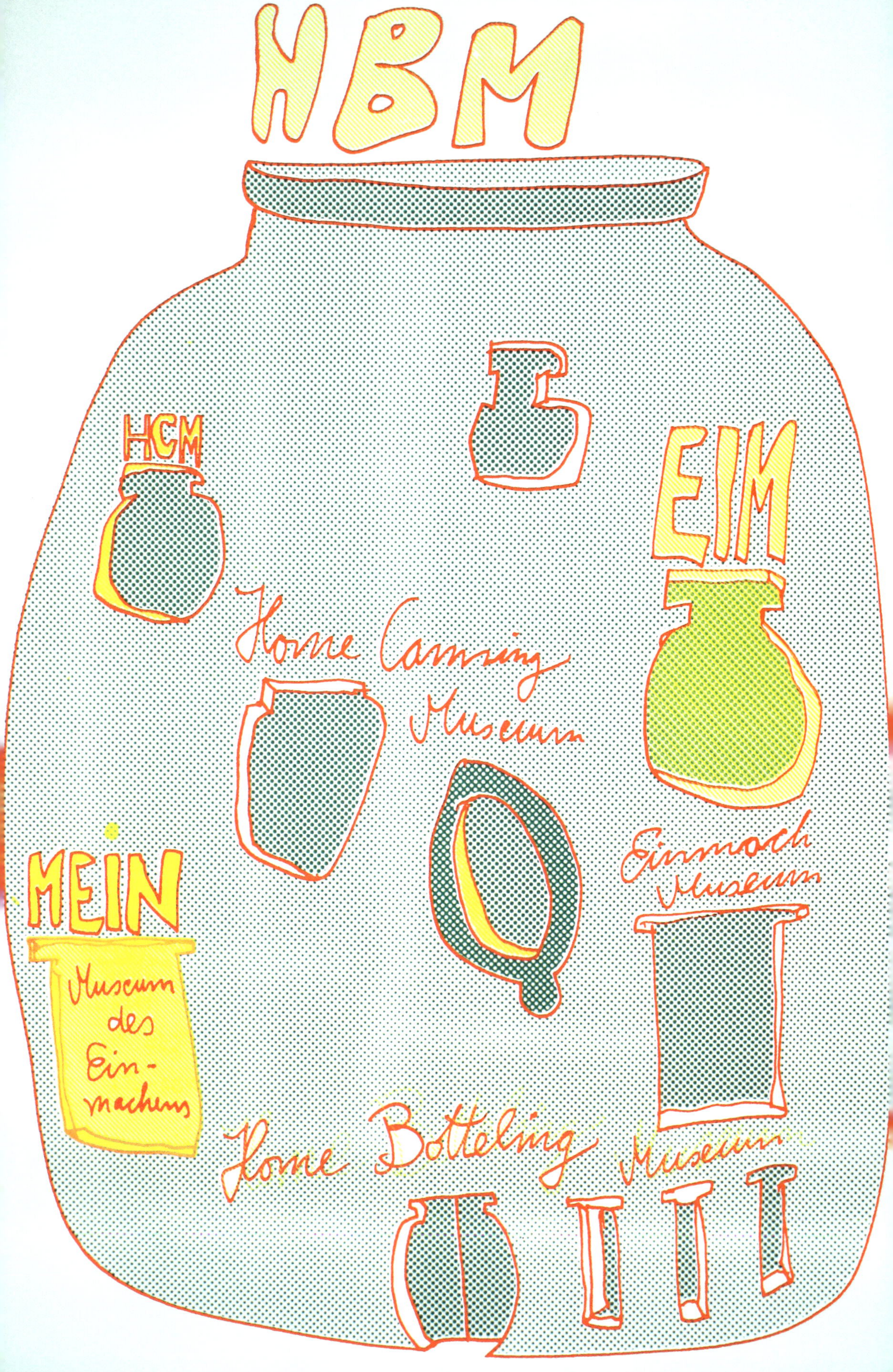
HBM
HCM
EIM
Home Canning Museum
MEIN
Museum des Ein-machens
Einmach Museum
Home Bottling Museum

Zdenka Badovinac

CARDBOARD BOX

One of the key terms of contemporary art is undoubtedly *white cube*, which is at present slowly being replaced by another term, namely *black box*. Regardless of the differences between them, they both seem to mean the same thing everywhere, both terms seemingly universal.

In my almost 20-year-long involvement in eastern European art and its history, I've permanently been faced with the problem of terms that, although they sounded the same, meant different things in different contexts. The meaning of individual terms has always been—still is—dependent on the perception of art and its contents in specific environments, as well as on the conditions of its production and presentation. For example, the term *white cube* in the malnourished eastern European art infrastructure was never that of the spotlessly white and illuminated museum, but more often yellowish or greyish, a slightly restless space, even, thanks to neon lights flickering somewhere. Likewise, the *black box* has never been completely dark, since light has always seeped through from somewhere, either through worn curtains or badly covered windows.

In addition to the poorly maintained buildings and the meagre funds for mounting exhibitions, the infrastructural underfunding of eastern European museums was noticeable in the insufficient historicization that has remained a huge problem until now.

When I was curating the exhibition *Body and the East* in 1989 the materials I collected during my travels mostly came directly from the artists, because at the time not much of the art of the post-war avant-garde had found its way into formal institutions. A similar thing happened in the years that followed, as I was collecting materials for our collection of eastern European art, *Arteast 2000+*, as well as for some other eastern European projects. The artists I met in the process provided not only the works for the exhibition, but also information about local histories not available in official sources: not just informal conversations, but documented facts, supported by the documents that the artists-archivists had been keeping in cardboard boxes in their homes for decades.

Artist's archive is another term that many people think means the same thing everywhere, but it does not. Even in the case of the different documents that artists subsequently exhibit in the format of artistic works, we have to say that both the motives of creating such archives and their functions differ. As early as 2006, when curating an exhibition called *Interrupted Histories* for the Museum of Modern Art in Ljubljana, I called the function of eastern European artist's archives "self-historicization", describing it thus:

Self-historicization is an informal system of historicization carried out by artists who, as a result of the absence of an adequate collective history, are forced to search for their own historical-interpretative context themselves. Because the local institutions that should have systematised post-war avant-garde art either didn't exist in the non-western world, or held such art in contempt, artists in certain regions found themselves compelled to collect archives of documents related to their own art, to the art of other artists, as well as to wider artistic movements and the conditions of their production. For younger artists now, this strategy of historicization takes on new forms, linked primarily to the critique of new social relationships which try to instrumentalize history. If, until recently, it was mostly post-war avant-gardes that were the subject of self-historicization, today, for example in the territories of former Yugoslavia, it is also the cultural legacy of Socialism and of the partisan movement.

My keyword *cardboard box* refers primarily to the generation of artists-archivists who collected documents about their work and the art of their local context in the 1960s and 1970s, mainly to retain its memory and begin the process of its informal historicization.

Since the beginning of the 1970s individual artists, such as Przemysław Kwiek and Zofia Kulik in Poland, György Galántai and Júlia Klaniczay in Hungary, have started to gather documentary materials about informal art. Lia Perjovschi has been doing the same in Romania since the 1980s.

The archive of the Polish artists Przemysław Kwiek and Zofia Kulik began in the early 1970s with the purpose of documenting informal art that was ephemeral and characterized by material instability. This way they preserved evidence about an important part of Polish art, which was marginalized by the official establishment, as well as documents on education in art academies and censorship. Nowadays this archive can be seen at numerous exhibitions in the form of an art installation.

Artpool, which has been maintained in Hungary since 1970 by György Galántai and Júlia Klaniczay and became an alternative art institution in 1979, has dedicated itself to informal art since its beginnings. Its founders have in different ways (particularly in Galántai's studio) given artists the chance to present and create new forms of art (conceptual art, mail art, visual poetry, kinetic art, land art, actions, happenings) that were not possible in the official art spaces of socialist Hungary at the time. Their multifaceted creativity has left us a unique archive that helps recreate the Hungarian neo-avant-garde art scene from the 1970s and 1980s.

In Romania, Lia Perjovschi has been creating her Contemporary Art Archive / Center for Art Analysis since 1985. She presents its archival materials in different ways; sometimes she appears as a detective searching through exhibited materials and documents to recover meanings, lost and hidden ideas, works, and artists from local, regional, and international cultural/artistic histories.

It is interesting to note how many artists-archivists are women, not only in eastern Europe, but also in Latin America. I would like to mention here that in my long involvement in eastern European art I've always been less interested in the question of a common European identity than in the common need to overcome bad conditions for the production, presentation, and distribution of art. Of course, this has never been solely an eastern European problem, as we found out when my colleagues and I, while working on these projects, started to work with more and more artists and curators from Latin America, because we found out that we shared many a common trait, both in the past, during the times of dictatorial regimes and isolation, and now. In the course of one such collaborations I met Graciela Carnevale.

Graciela Carnevale was a member of the Grupo de Arte de Vanguardia de Rosario, a collective that, among other things, organized a legendary artistic and political action, *Tucumán Arde* (1968), and whose documents were held by the artist—along with the documents of other avant-garde actions, for example her legendary performance *Encierro* (Confinement,1968). For decades, Carnevale has kept the growing archive in her home; however, only after 1990 did the public start to take an interest in it.

Besides the invaluable importance of this archive and its self-historicization, it is also interesting and instructive to note how the artist decided to upgrade the original location of her archive to a cardboard box. Of course, the actual boxes and binders that initially housed the archive are not so important. The format of a cardboard box here serves as a metaphor of the private context and self-historicization. On the initiative of the Espaivisor Gallery in Valencia, Graciela Carnevale recently agreed to create an edition of her archive in neat grey boxes of various sizes, now available for exhibitions and purchase. The gallery managed to persuade the artist by arguing that the sales could generate the funds necessary to keep the archive in Argentina, purchase a suitable permanent location and obtain funds for its digitalization.

Artist's archives of eastern European and Latin American artists serve a different function than those in the western world, which can rely on a richer and more developed cultural infrastructure. After providing tools for the historicization of informal art under authoritarian regimes, these archives are now struggling to preserve evidence of local traditions in the countries where they were created; they are also contributing to the development of the cultural infrastructure that is now being built in many places, as well as of the symbolic capital with which we're just entering the global exchange of ideas.

A cardboard box is thus becoming a symbol of the decolonization of knowledge and of the re-activation of marginalized positions in global communication.

Annemarie Matzke /
She She Pop

SCHUBLADEN

DRAWERS

After my grandmother died, I found among her things three postcards that are strangely similar. They had been sent in different decades by different people she knew. All three are picture postcards showing the interiors of communal rooms in recreational facilities for the different public bodies of the German nation ("Volkskörper").

In all three, there are small tables with chairs arranged neatly around them. In all three, the chairs are empty. In all three, the rooms are decorated with cut flowers or plants. In each room, there are pictures hanging on the walls. On the oldest postcard, there is a portrait of Adolf Hitler on the back wall. The second shows Willi Stoph and Erich Honecker hanging side by side. On the last one, we can vaguely make out a kind of landscape painting, like the pictures hanging in doctors' surgeries. What astonished me so much in my discovery was that these three cultural systems, which were so different, could ultimately blend into the same image—and how this ended up in my grandmother's drawer.

(Lisa Lucassen speaking in the performance *Schubladen*, 2012)

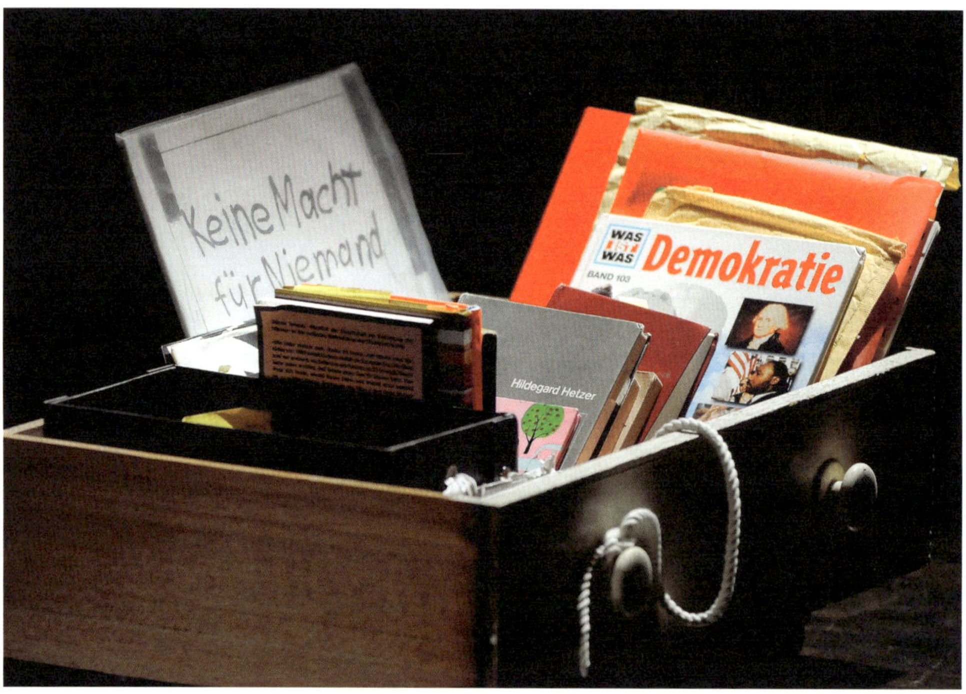

When we open a drawer, we find a special kind of archive. Whether the drawer reveals chaos or is organized according to a careful sorting system, all the things we find inside have one thing in common: they were put there because they were meant for keeping, but also to be kept out of sight. They are not deemed meaningful enough to be hung on a wall, placed in a showcase, or set on a dresser. They are deemed important and should be at hand, but not necessarily all the time. They are things that we do not want to, or need to, be reminded of every day. Drawers also offer us a glimpse into the relationship between the drawer archivists and their history, for they represent a desire to control or suppress. Inspecting a drawer may reveal a tidy person who likes to systematize things and assign value to them. Then again, we may find chaos—things lying willy-nilly side by side; things that only share in common the fact that they are thought to be worth keeping. The drawer archive consists of things that the archivist does not want to deal with right away. It is a special kind of archive that can be found anywhere and is easily overlooked. Yet, emptying a drawer often evokes strong emotions (comparable to a purse, but if a purse stands for short-term memory, then the drawer archive stands for long-term memory).

So, what happens when three women who grew up in West Germany open the drawers of their childhood and youth, together with three women who were socialized in East Germany and who have also brought their private archives along with them? What happens when books, letters, songs, films, and diaries that were stored and long forgotten, hidden from view in different drawers, are taken out, and an attempt is made to reconstruct the historical context to which they belong?

In the performance *Schubladen* (Drawers), we—the performance group She She Pop—present our drawer archives as a way of talking about and questioning our own personal history of the German separation. Each drawer serves as a material collection, the content of which is examined on stage in front of an audience and in the presence of the "partner" performer from the other part of Germany.

Each performer enters the stage with her drawer on wheels. These personal, mobile archives full of books, audio cassettes, photo albums, school books, and letters are the starting point for the performance. The performers reach into their drawers and take out memorable objects, using these as a basis for telling individual stories and narrating collective history. At each table, two people sit facing each other. One performer is from East Germany, while the other has grown up in West Germany. In all, there are six pairs who represent East-West German history, each with their own individual memories. Between them, the pile of objects from their mobile archives—their drawers—continues to grow, taking the shape of a perplexing collection of materials, which they use as a basis for talking about their socialization as women in the two different parts of Germany. The fundamental question is this: how did they become the women they are today? Personal things are brought out into the open and presented in all their uniqueness.

History materializes in the objects they show to each other and to the audience. Books are read aloud, diary entries are rediscovered, songs are played on the record player. Childcare books and schoolbooks are quoted, making palpable the different ideologies of child rearing and education. Love letters are read aloud and sex-education books exhibited. The relationship between personal history and social history comes to the fore.

This is only one aspect of the archives that are presented, however. The objects not only relay history, they can also be experienced in their materiality. Letters or diary entries are more than just texts read aloud; they are objects that display their own specific character. Letters are taken out of envelopes; records are inseparable from their covers; the binding of a diary shows that it holds many entries. The objects are passed from one performer to the next.

Objects are made visible and tangible by being used. A record player stands on the table. We observe the act of putting on a record. The static produced by each record played makes the past audible. Each object becomes part of a person's history, and its narration is connected to the bodies of the performers. This is because the objects are not just shown; they are touched, too, held in hands. Each time a performer reaches for a book, she is making a choice. Memory is thus not only what can be told, but also what needs to be understood and used. New traces of passing time are added to those that time has already left on the objects, meaning that the archive is presented as incomplete. What is shown here is the processual character of the act of archiving and remembering. Memory is not just told, it is literally made palpable and passed on.

At first glance, the things retrieved from the drawers appear random. The seemingly incoherent collection of materials interrogates history in a new way. The past, a decisive break, a dramatic moment, is relived through the archived objects. At stake here are issues such as loss and separation and how these are represented through objects. It is a story held together only through the personal narrations and the bodies of the performers.

Everything is placed on the tables. In the course of the evening, these collected materials grow into mountains, as the emptied drawer archives fill the stage bit by bit. What is marginal, peripheral, banal, neglected, or too private is juxtaposed with overarching questions of political ideologies and contemporary history. In this staged East-West German dialogue, the archived texts weave together to form a common narrative that cannot be separated from the bodies and emotions of performers and audience alike. In the end, the drawers are empty, while the stage is full of things that have revealed a personal history. By the end of the evening, an ephemeral and subjective archive has been created—a personal museum of recent German history.

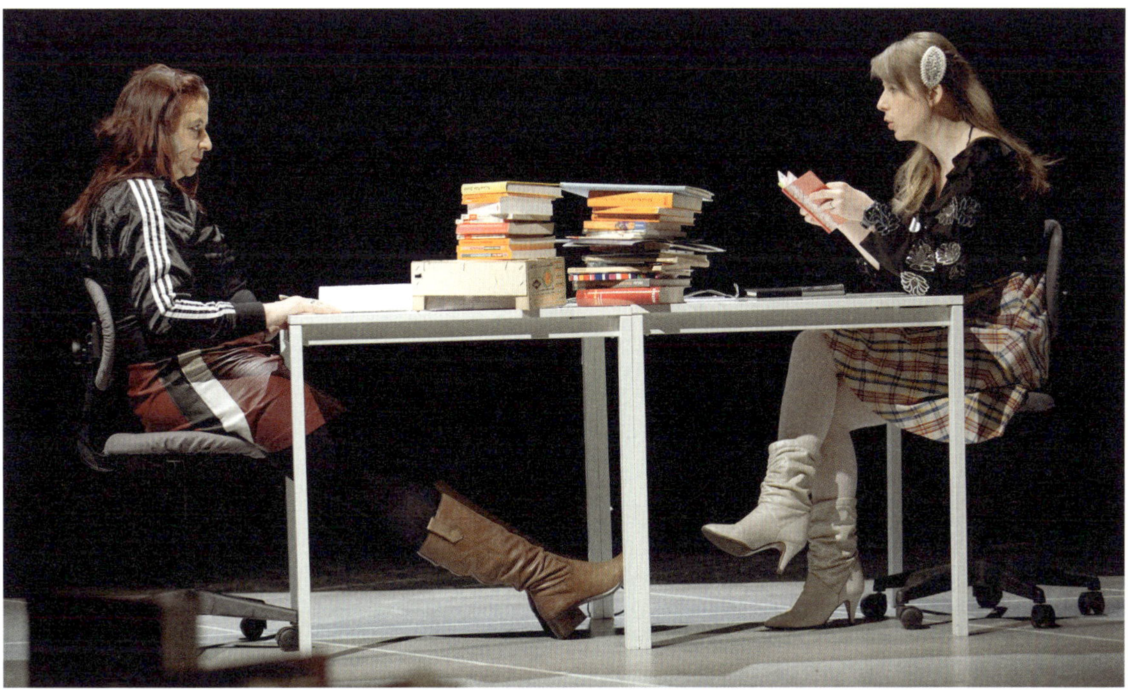

Tim Etchells

INDEX CARDS

Before 2001 I kept a series of notebooks in which I collected short texts: ideas, notes, lists, and phrases of my own linguistic invention alongside fragments from overheard conversations, movies, newspapers, and books. Effectively a scrapbook of fragments that interested me for one undefined reason or another, these were materials flagged for later use or investigation, oddities, and half-thoughts, accumulated in haphazard fashion. That said, it was in these notebooks that ideas for my projects or writing often first surfaced, their pages containing the seeds for things that might one day play their part in performance texts, fiction, or other kinds of projects. As well as a tool—a place to start or perhaps a place to go to when stuck or searching for a new way forward—the notebooks were also, inevitably, a kind of personal archive, an irregular collection of materials—not a diary in any commonly understood sense, but tied nonetheless to the passage of time, building day by day, and week by week, growing in a tangential relation to the things that I did, thought, felt, and saw, if only from the corner of my eye.

Sometime in 2001 I pretty much gave up working in these physical notebooks, switching instead to a "Notes" Word file on my laptop, which served the same function whilst allowing for a simple cut-and-paste-in of materials from websites, emails, or other electronic documents. Making my notes directly digital also afforded an easier trajectory for texts I was intent on working with in my writing projects, since they could simply be copied and pasted straight into place. The stages of my previous process—handwriting notes from a printed or digital source in order to later key them into the computer for work—was happily simplified: cut, paste.

The "Notes" file on my laptop now stretches to 300 pages or so and its contents mirror those of the physical notebooks I used to keep. It's a place to record things and a place to go when looking for inspiration for projects, or when looking for particular kinds of materials that I might need. The file is searchable, so if I can remember a word combination from a fragment I'm looking for, I can easily locate it. Like the physical notebooks, the "Notes" file is also a kind of timeline, with original entries at the bottom and new materials added line by line to the top, each new addition pushing older materials further and further down as a kind of linguistic sediment. From time to time a date appears in the text—a co-ordinate by which to understand the location of things, their place in life or other narratives—but mostly

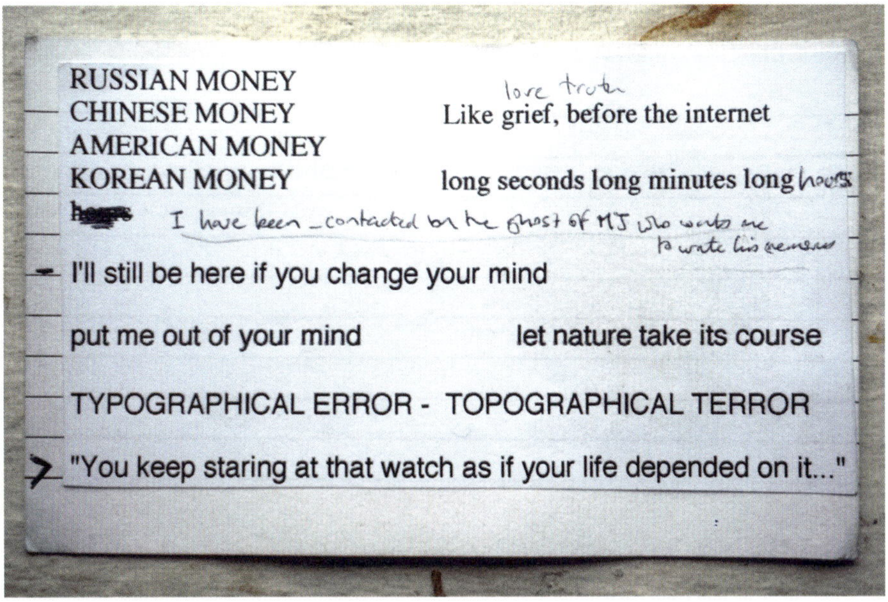
RUSSIAN MONEY
CHINESE MONEY
AMERICAN MONEY
KOREAN MONEY
love truth
Like grief, before the internet
long seconds long minutes long hours
I have been contacted by the ghost of MJ
I'll still be here if you change your mind
put me out of your mind
let nature take its course
TYPOGRAPHICAL ERROR - TOPOGRAPHICAL TERROR
"You keep staring at that watch as if your life depended on it..."

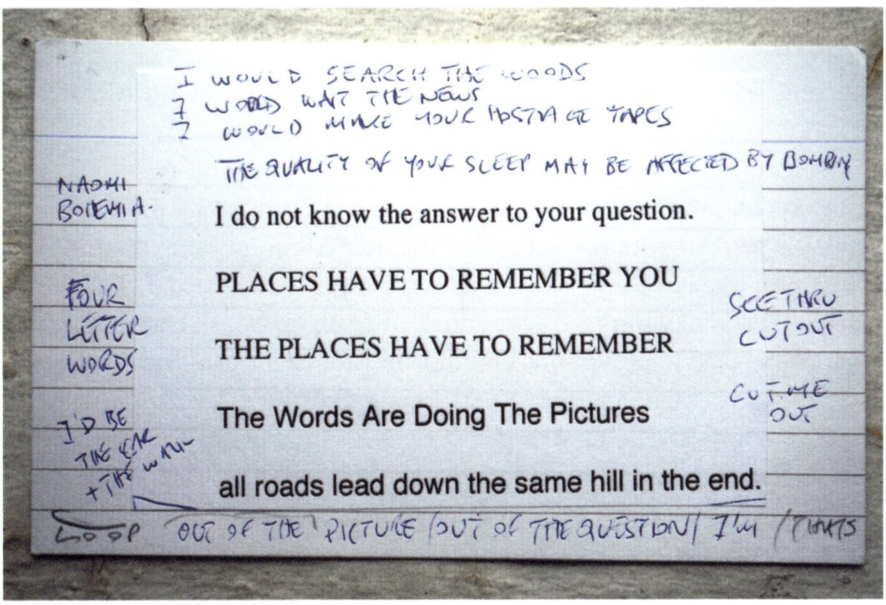
I WOULD SEARCH THE WOODS
I WOULD MAKE YOUR HOSTAGE TAPES
THE QUALITY OF YOUR SLEEP MAY BE AFFECTED BY BOMBING
BOHEMIA.
I do not know the answer to your question.
FOUR LETTER WORDS
PLACES HAVE TO REMEMBER YOU
SEE THRU CUT OUT
THE PLACES HAVE TO REMEMBER
CUT ME OUT
I'D BE THE CAR + THE WALL
The Words Are Doing The Pictures
all roads lead down the same hill in the end.
LOOP OUT OF THE PICTURE / OUT OF THE QUESTION / I'M

the fragments appear without a reference to the context from which they were sampled—"pieces of language" taken out of place and left in storage.

In late 2013, aware that much of the contents of my "Notes" file typically remains unused and unseen by anyone but me, I started work on a performance project called *A Broadcast / Looping Pieces*, with the explicit motivation of exploring and reacting to material collected over the years. The form for this work was a kind of rolling improvisation, a performance in which I would scan the notebook for text to read, selecting fragments which I'd then repeat, loop, alter, and join with each other in different combinations.

This work had its origin in other aspects of my practice over many years, but was informed by two experimental processes that I undertook earlier in 2013.

In the first of these—realized in the framework of an event called *Brouillon*, curated by Boris Charmatz at the gallery Argos in Brussels—I worked in relation to two works on video by other artists, finding different ways of animating a relation to them through language; in one case extending or parsing the work into spoken word performance, and in the other reworking, remixing, and composing the text already present to make new text-drawings and spoken word improvisations in response to its materials.

In the second of the experiments that led to my *A Broadcast / Looping Pieces*, I worked with the sound artist Tarek Atoui, inviting him into the frame of a large-scale Forced Entertainment project, titled *The Last Adventures*, and beginning a discussion on the rule-and-task based modes of composition and improvisation common to Atoui's musical endeavours and the company's own practice in performance. Atoui's *Metastable Circuit* (2012) comprised a computational system (or instrument) designed to access the entire database of his sound archive, breaking, compounding, and combining tiny slithers of the recordings and feeding these to Atoui in real time as a constantly shifting improvisation material and challenge. Atoui's construction—a device intended to surprise him—ensures his encounter with the unexpected and the unfamiliar, and closely parallels the kinds of non-computational structures that we've explored in Forced Entertainment's work to related ends. The result in each case is a negotiation between a triumvirate of forces—known or fixed elements, unexpected or unfamiliar elements, and finally, performer intuition.

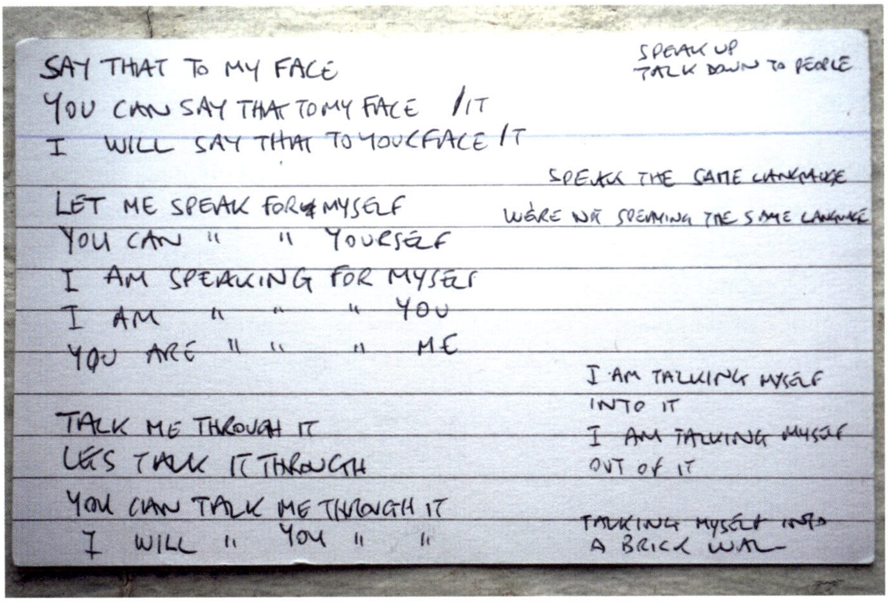
SAY THAT TO MY FACE
YOU CAN SAY THAT TO MY FACE /IT
I WILL SAY THAT TO YOUR FACE /IT
SPEAK UP
TALK DOWN TO PEOPLE
SPEAK THE SAME LANGUAGE
WE'RE NOT SPEAKING THE SAME LANGUAGE
LET ME SPEAK FOR MYSELF
YOU CAN " " YOURSELF
I AM SPEAKING FOR MYSELF
I AM " " " YOU
YOU ARE " " " ME
I AM TALKING MYSELF INTO IT
I AM TALKING MYSELF OUT OF IT
TALK ME THROUGH IT
LET'S TALK IT THROUGH
YOU CAN TALK ME THROUGH IT
I WILL " YOU " "
TALKING MYSELF INTO A BRICK WALL

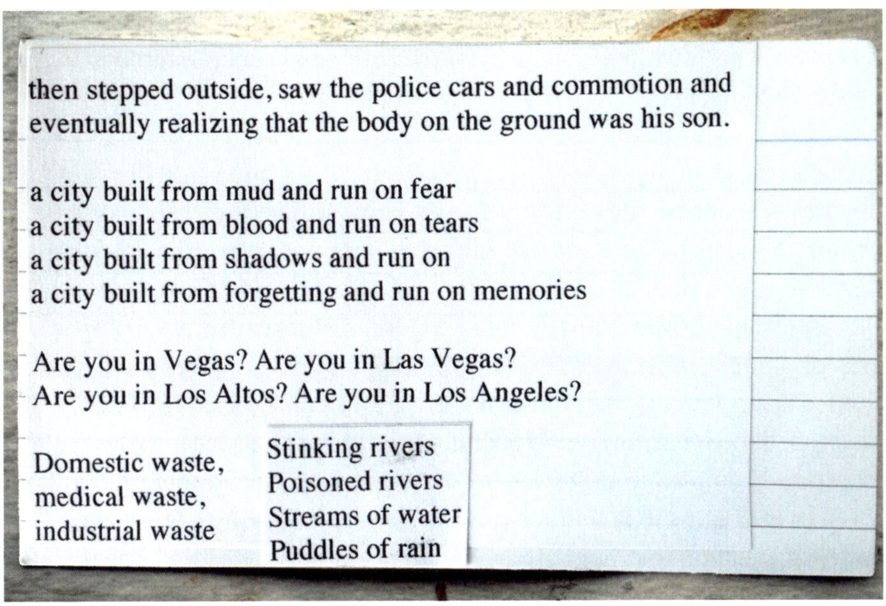
then stepped outside, saw the police cars and commotion and eventually realizing that the body on the ground was his son.
a city built from mud and run on fear
a city built from blood and run on tears
a city built from shadows and run on
a city built from forgetting and run on memories
Are you in Vegas? Are you in Las Vegas?
Are you in Los Altos? Are you in Los Angeles?
Domestic waste,
medical waste,
industrial waste
Stinking rivers
Poisoned rivers
Streams of water
Puddles of rain

Throughout the work on *The Last Adventures*, I was wondering what a textual equivalent to Atoui's *Metastable Circuit* might be, especially in the sense that the project combined the realities of archive, or database, and of instrument. Realizing that my equivalent to Atoui's database of recorded sounds and samples was probably the Word "Notes" file on my computer, I began to think about ways of working with this material as an element in an improvised but decidedly more low-fi performance built around looping, reordering, and combining previously collected or written fragments of language. It was there, in that set of thoughts, that my work on *A Broadcast / Looping Pieces* began.

Accepting an invitation from Tilmann Broszat to perform in Munich in December 2013, I worked on animating my own notebook as database, archive, and improvisational instrument, and suggested the title *A Broadcast / Looping Pieces*. In preparation for the first performance, I printed the Word document of my notes and spread the resulting pages across a series of tables. Improvising from these materials, I used single lines, phrases, and paragraphs, glimpsed on or read from the papers, looping and jumping from one piece of material to another, much as I had done when working with text taken from the videos I'd encountered at Argos earlier in the year.

Focusing now on my own notes, and on an investigation into the rhythms, textures, semantics, and performative dynamics of the text, I soon discarded certain elements of the notes that inhibited improvisation, especially longer, discursive, or extended narrative forms. I also began to make links across the timeframe of the notes, joining together phrases from very different eras or contexts, discovering new connections and productive disconnections. Performing the material aloud in various contexts since Munich, I've developed the piece further—radically reworking and rewriting text in live improvisation—sometimes letting new word choices appear at random through the high-speed delivery and sometimes allowing tiredness or slippages of attention to produce mistakes, slips of the tongue, and free association to play a part in the construction and development of the performance.

After working with text fragments printed on A4 pages for a while, I started using index cards as a better physical form/home for the fragmented and playful process that characterizes *Broadcast*. I made the choice for pragmatic reasons; the index cards were robust, easy to handle and shuffle, easy to carry in one hand, and not too bulky. They had a surface area that could accommodate a moderate amount of text, making it easy, in the performance situation, to survey a range of options at a glance; but, at the same time, the cards were not *too* large either, so as to contain too much text in which the eye might get lost whilst scanning options.

In many ways the index cards represent a kind of retrograde mutation in the form of my text; as functional and necessary items they are nonetheless props, and return the writing to an analogue (printed) schema after a 14-year spell as digital native. Interestingly, the index cards are of course no index at all, as they don't refer to any actual or viable frame of conceptual or semantic organization; rather, their form floats the spectre of organization whilst providing only a system of division and subdivision. Containing fragments for reorganization, the cards are simply larger and endlessly re-deployable fragments themselves, shifting indices of their own—in any case, fluid—contents.

Paul Clarke

STEWARD

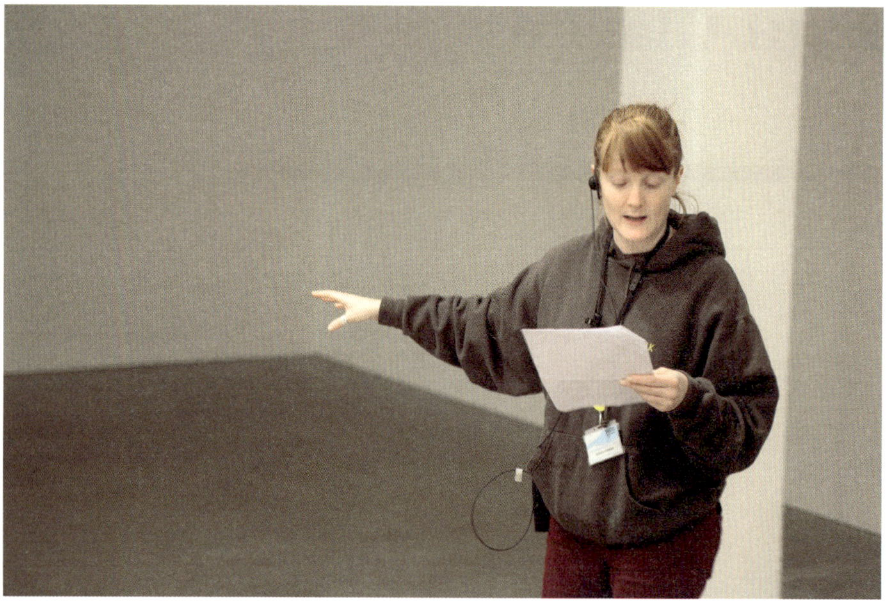

Here is how the Gallery 1 steward, Jess Robins, describes the absent film work by Kerry Tribe, *H.M.* (2009):

There is a white-painted room built in the gallery here. Two 16mm film projectors point through two rectangular holes in the wall. There are a few metres between them. The same film spools from one projector to the other. The 2 projections are side by side. On the left you see a black and white image of Yuri Gagarin, the first man in space, and on the right the date 1961. There's a 20 second delay between the projectors and after 20 seconds Gagarin appears on the right. He is replaced on the left by a headshot of an elderly man with grey hair brushed back, gold-rimmed glasses and a moustache. This is an interview with H.M., a man who had a large portion of his temporal lobe, at the front of his brain, excised in 1953, to control his massive epileptic seizures. After the operation he suffered severe amnesia, forgetting events as soon as they were out of his sight and mind. He could only remember for around 20 seconds. If you were to leave the room and re-enter he would not remember you. As the film concludes, the voice-over says, "What would it be like to live without recourse to the past? To lose the fourth dimension of time and live in the three dimensions of space alone?"

In 2012, Performance Re-enactment Society (PRS) presented *Group Show* at Arnolfini, Bristol, UK. This was an intangible exhibition, displayed through performance, with all four galleries empty of objects and the walls left white. The PRS curated *Group Show* from an imaginary permanent collection comprising all the visual art and performance that had been shown at Arnolfini since it was founded in 1961. There were three parts, each of which intervened in different ways in the archive, galleries, and institution. The first was made by Tom Marshman and took visitors behind the scenes, through a private door and into the intimate context of one of the dressing rooms. This aspect drew on interviews with technicians and performers' memories, about late-night installs and their preparations for shows at the art centre. The second was a series of performance interventions by Clare Thornton and Laura Dannequin, which took place in the galleries. Clare and Laura worked with paper-based documents of exhibitions from Arnolfini's archive as scores for choreography and movement, embodying past works, mostly sculpture. I will focus on the third part of *Group Show* that I curated, which was performed by the gallery's stewards and took the form of an exhibit in words.

I was inspired by browsing Arnolfini's slide collection, held by the Bristol Record Office, which was uncatalogued at the time, and is yet to be digitized. Pulling open the wooden drawers I encountered these slides organized arbitrarily into alphabetical order and roughly sorted by exhibition with handwritten stickers, some peeling away or fading. Researcher Cara Davies and I laid them out on a light box to attempt to figure out what they were of, whose works they represented, and which show they were from. We worked between these and brochures from the Arnolfini archive, also cross-referencing catalogues. We used magnifying glasses, photographed or scanned the slides, and blew them up to try to get at more detail. For recent exhibitions we accessed the institution's server, browsing unedited, raw jpeg files dumped in folders, which may have been dated but were not always labelled with the names of the shows they documented.

Rather than seeking chronological order I started to sort the slides on the light box and the photos or scans on screen according to visual motifs, grouping them into thematic collections, by recurrent materials or tropes. Next we transcribed the images of the artworks selected, translating them into written descriptions. This exercise in ekphrasis attempted to recreate works of art in words, depicting them in figurative language. Or, more precisely, these mimetic writings were responses to the slides and digital stills that documented these artworks as displayed in Arnolfini exhibitions. Ekphrasis was an anachronistic practice to apply in this context, more often used as an art-historical method where there are gaps in the record, common in early periods, rather than where photographic reproductions survive. Somewhere between the tiny 35mm slides and other documents that remained we tried to re-stage the exhibitions, to imagine being there amongst the objects shown, how we might have been affected by the chosen work in the context of the show and what it may have meant to us. In the case of some recent exhibitions, which we had seen, we also drew on our memories and the experiences the stewards we were collaborating with had of invigilating the work. One of the things we spoke about was that exhibitions, although they last longer than performances, with three or more months between their beginning and end, are still events with a limited duration, during which many ephemeral interactions take place between visitors and artworks, and with those stewarding.

I was interested in pictures becoming words and in these written texts being spoken, transformed into oral history and disseminated face-to-face. On entering Gallery 1, visitors were greeted by one of the stewards, Jess Robins, who said, "Hello. This is *Group Show* by Performance Re-enactment Society, would you like me to tell you about the work?". Rather than fulfilling the conventional gallery invigilator's role of offering explanations and interpreting the art on display, she described a series of works that had previously been shown at Arnolfini but were not there. The dramaturgy of her gallery tour traced associative motifs, rather than a critical or chronological narrative. The selection brought together works from different periods in the institution's development and art history, by artists who were not originally shown together. The impossible retrospective exhibition I curated included sculptures, paintings, photographs, video, installation, and performance works; these forms were shown both alongside one another and overlaid in the same place. Further narratives unfolded upstairs in Galleries 2, 3, and 4, performed by Fraisia Dunn, Katarina Complova, and Stella Thompson, all regular gallery stewards who had volunteered to participate.

Where invigilators are often invisible, ignored, and given little agency in the art institution, here the exhibition only took place through visitors engaging with them. Their acts of speaking the art were performative, making these absent works appear, remade differently as images in each listener's imagination, which they could project onto the white walls and bare concrete floors of the galleries. For frequent Arnolfini visitors, certain descriptions triggered memories of seeing exhibitions; their memories mingled with the invigilators' words, and they also interjected themselves. The invigilators became the keepers of a special collection, stewarding descriptions of past exhibitions and works, keeping them alive by speaking them in a new performance, resisting their historicization by gesturing towards where they once were, which constituted a form of appearance. This group exhibition was composed of immaterial art objects, but objects nonetheless.

Małgorzata Szczęśniak

BIEL

WHITENESS

1 Disappearing whiteness

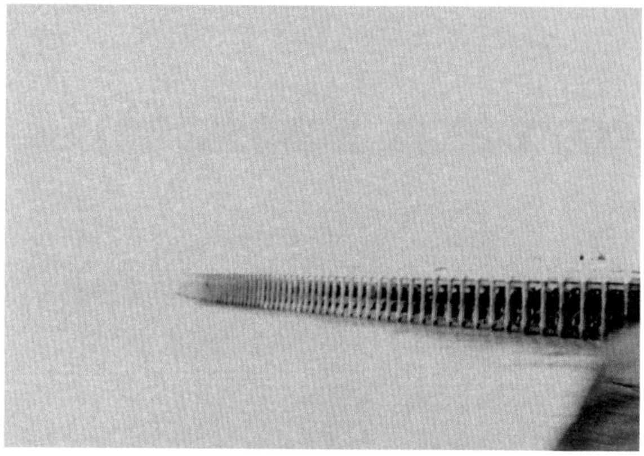

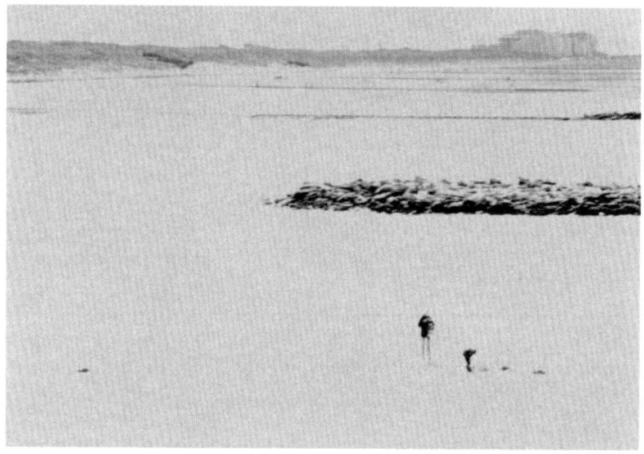

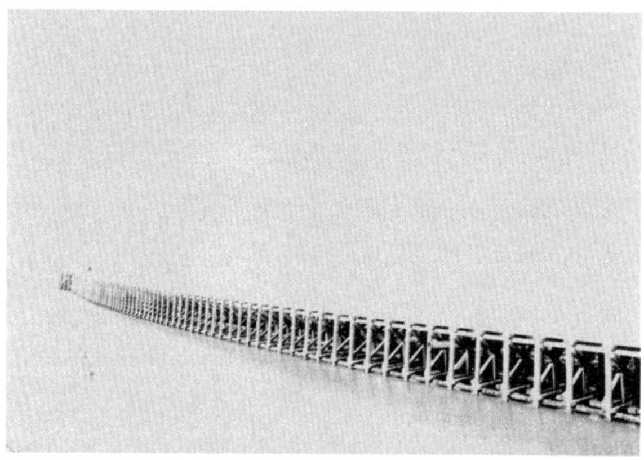

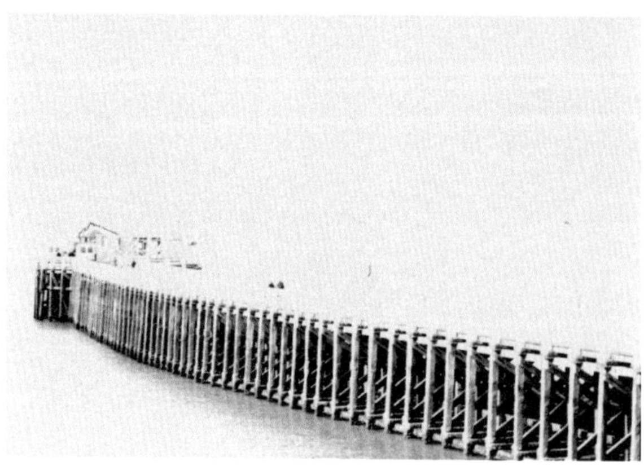

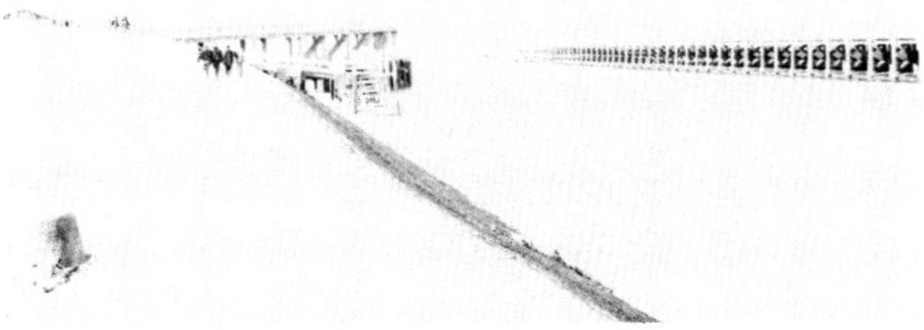

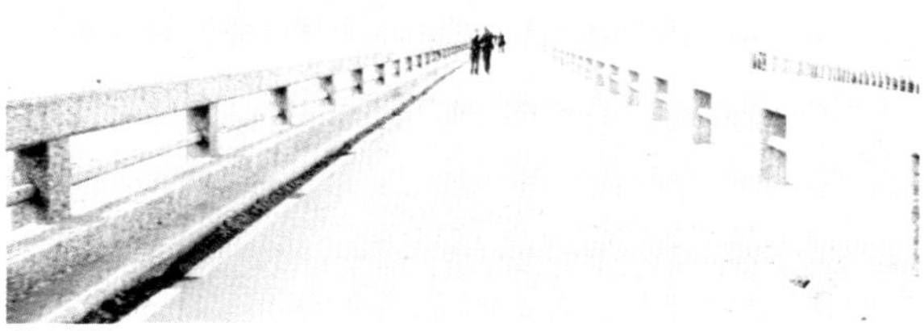

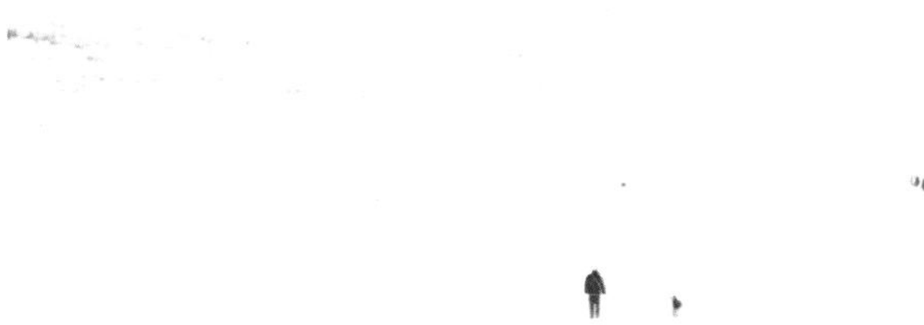

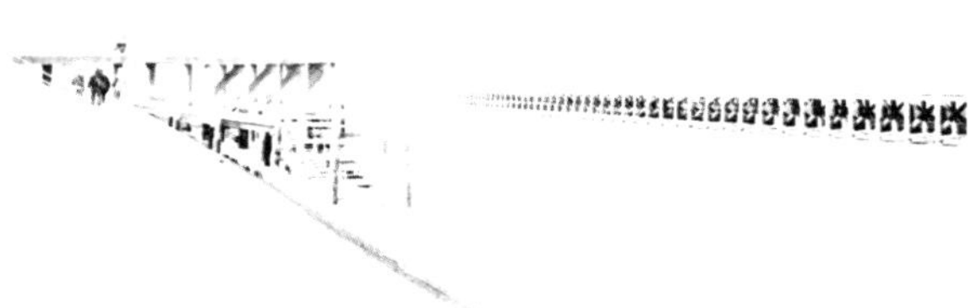

2
Travelling in search of lost time

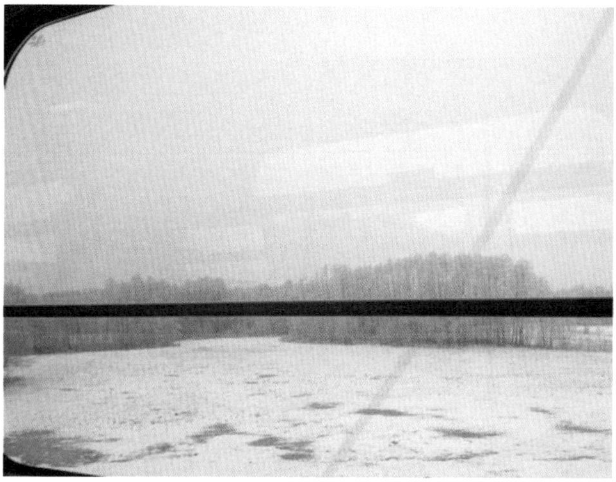

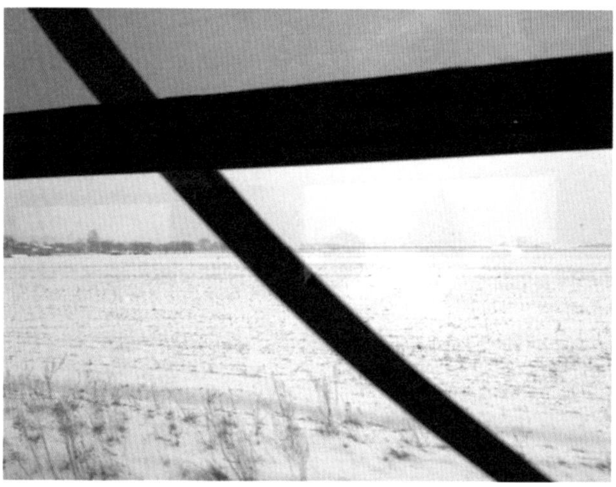

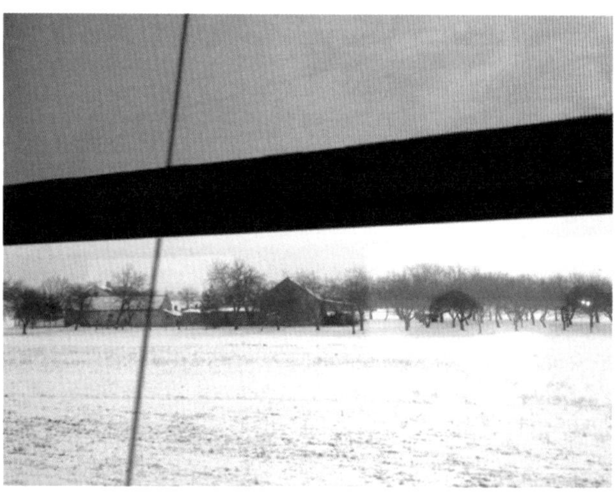

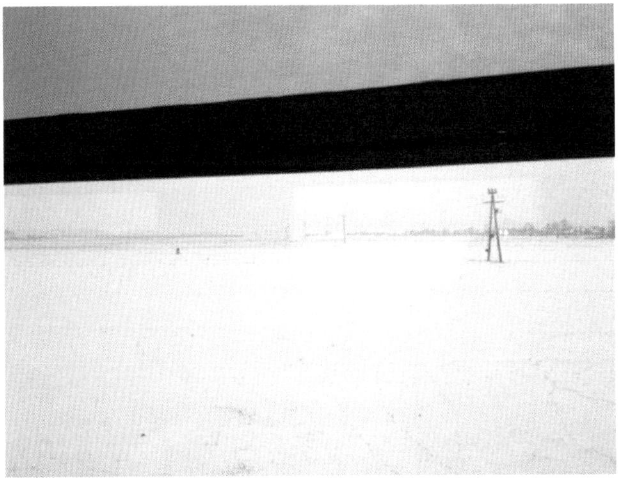

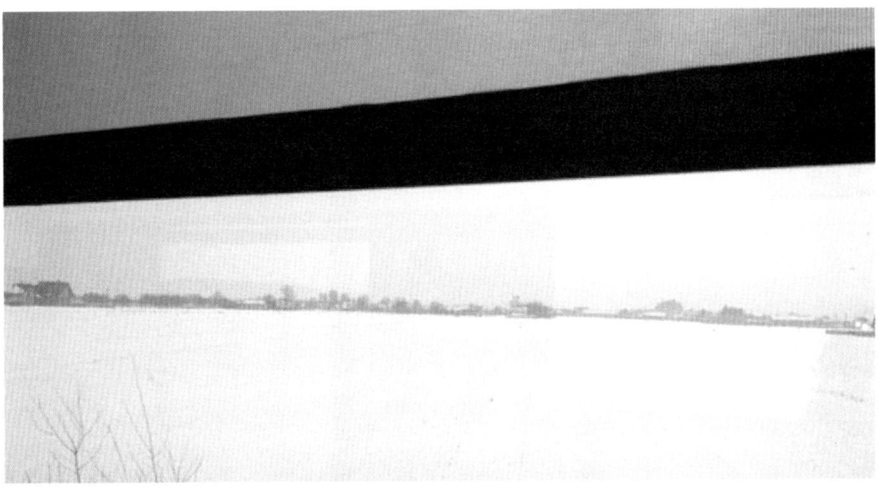

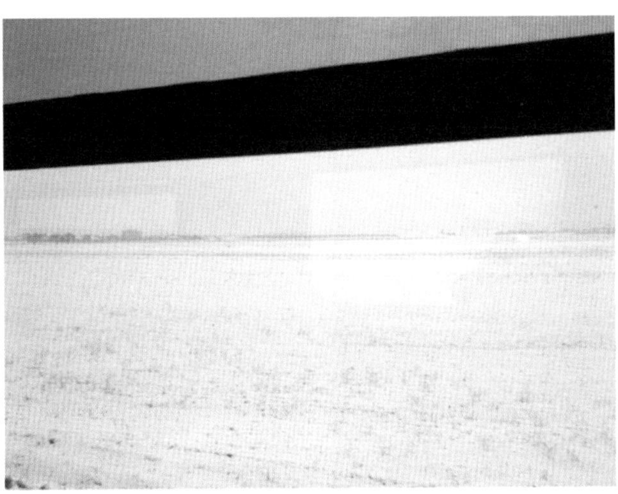

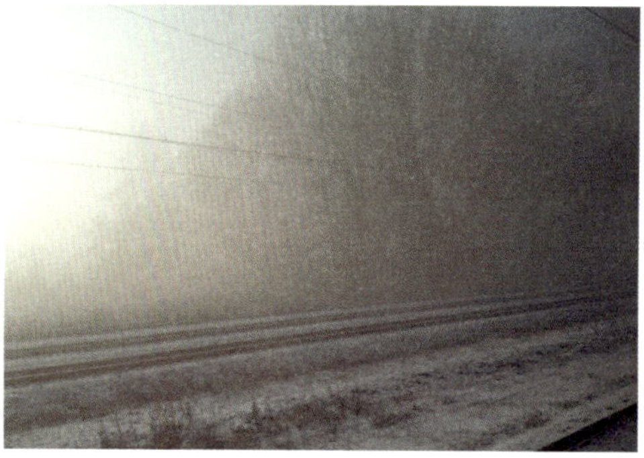

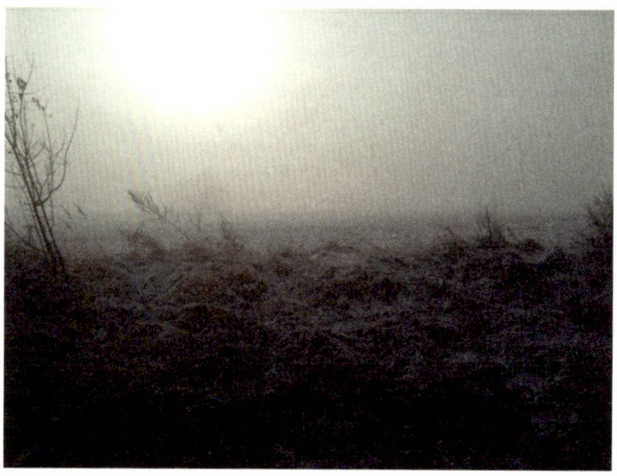

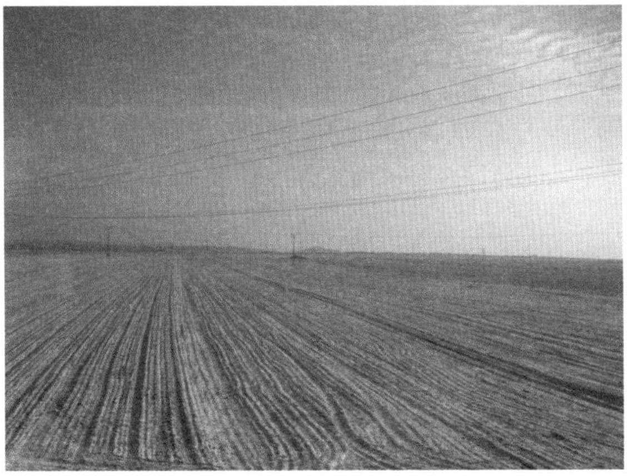

That disappearing whiteness, that pull into the North Sea, some seaside town, Northern Belgium, or rather Flanders.

A weird time, so tired, everything would disappear from before my eyes, a recording of my condition as reflected in a catastrophic perception. This cycle develops enormously, but what matters most is that you disappear, dissolve into the whiteness as the fog envelops you.

You see details that become a vision of the apocalyptic nature of your thoughts. It was cold, cold wind and silver air, like in Flanders. That's when I understood Flemish paintings, those silver particles in the air, shimmering, a horizon without lines, just quivering and vibrating air.

A very acoustic sensation of whiteness. The whiteness disappears, changing into the vibration of thoughts and air. It fills a horizon that's not there.

time wrapped up in a white paper sheet

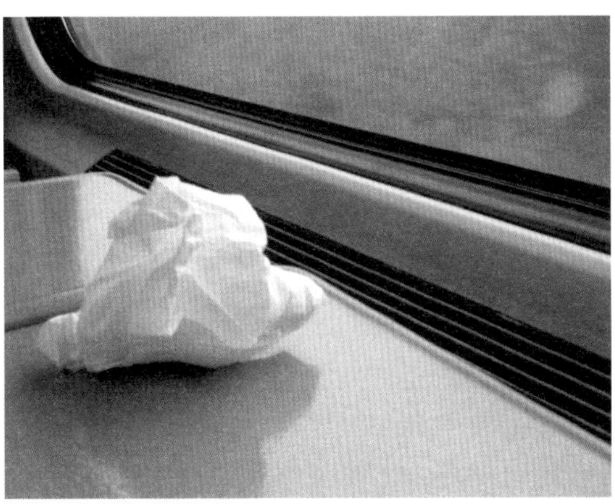

3

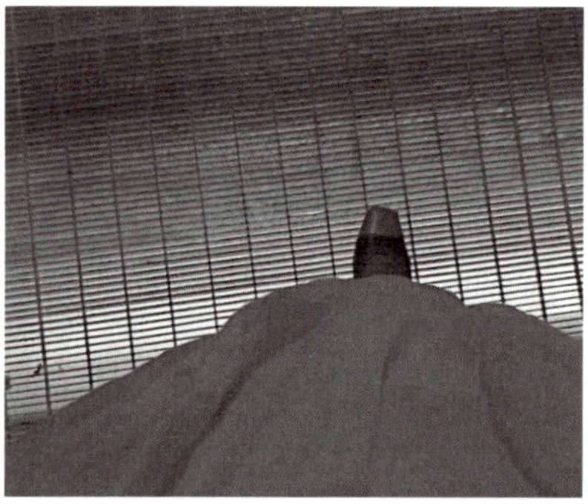

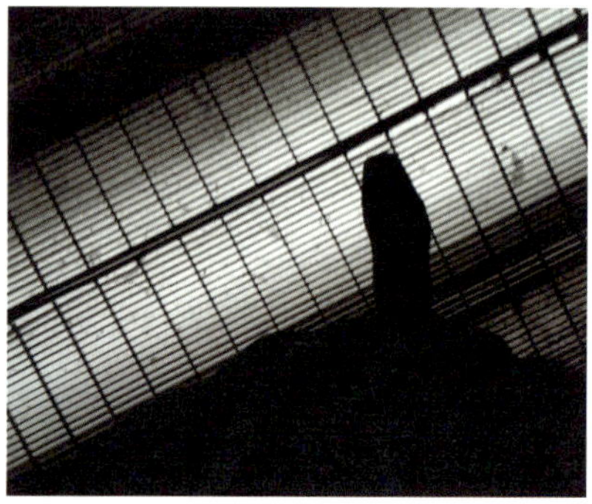

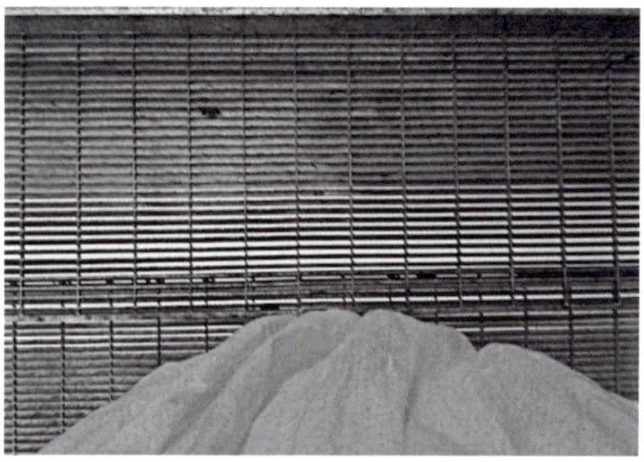

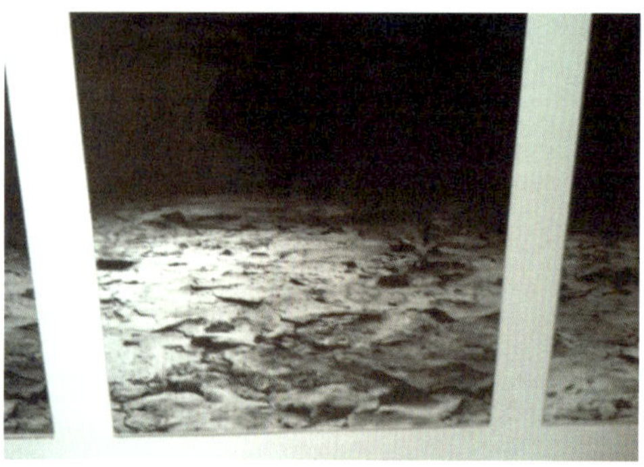

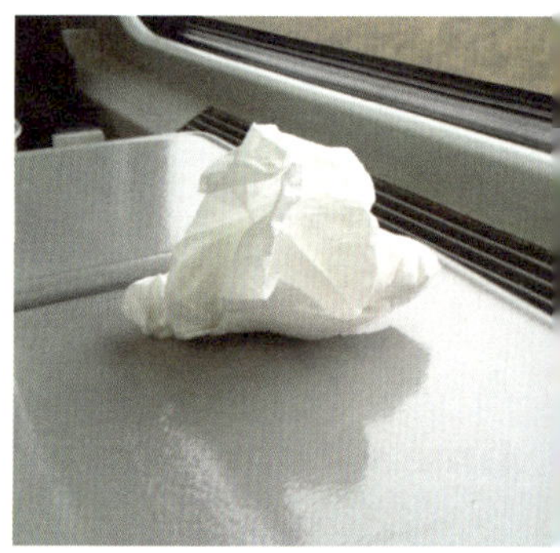

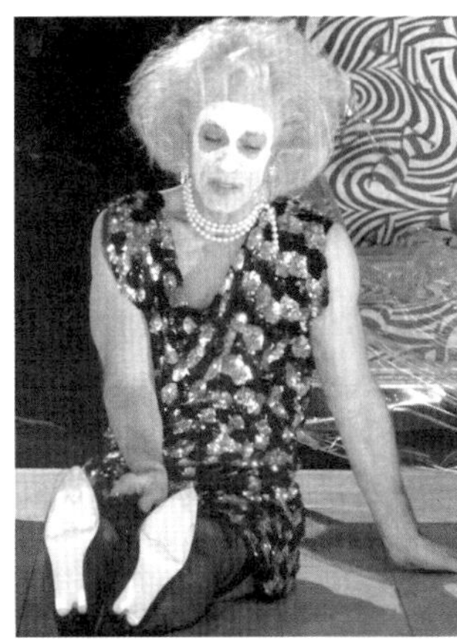

Małgorzata Dziewulska

DRZAZGI

SPLINTERS

My archive comes from a place that is completely real. It has its own daily routine that repeats itself in the usual way, like everywhere else. Yet the order of this invisible life contains certain unspoken things that remain pushed to the side, perhaps forgotten. They resemble splinters, in that they only reveal themselves on occasion and are otherwise manageable in our everyday lives. These unexposed contents of our individual and collective lives, contents hidden beneath the surface, are the cause of the cyclical collection and collapse, integration and dispersal of my archive. Archives are not arranged by meaning, however, but according to formal criteria such as date, source, and format. The important is shelved alongside the less important. How do we accommodate the internal shifts that blur the shape of my catalogue, turning it into a collection of "who knows what"?

1. Palatino linotype

I must start by introducing the archive of Roman Lipa. Born in 1923, Lipa finished elementary school, but his parents could not afford to educate him further. He became a carpenter and later a photographer. By the time he started a family, he owned 1.61 hectares of land. He also worked as a firefighter and luthier. His war story is one of illegal enterprises: escapes, stints in jail, living in hiding, participating in the underground resistance, and fighting in a Home Army platoon. After the war Lipa took up painting, and later had many exhibitions. His love for painting was linked to his passion for chronicling; he claimed to enjoy depicting old events that could no longer be documented with a camera. He wrote a history of his village, compiling earlier notes into the books *Refugees*, a memoir of September 1939, *A Diary of the Occupation*, and *From Our Past*. He was not the only one to document local history, but his work stood out in its respect for the facts, the attention it paid to individuals, and its impartiality. Lipa died recently, and his writings remain unpublished. His granddaughter has transcribed them on a computer.

in the archive

Landscapes are either remembered, photographed, or painted by Lipa. The former ones are fragmentary and inconstant; they belong to the already mentioned disorder in the the collection, unlike Lipa's paintings, which exactly portray that particular fragment of Subcarpathia. The miniature effect of this landscape derives not only from the configuration of the land, but also from the thick segmentation into triangles and rhombuses. Here the

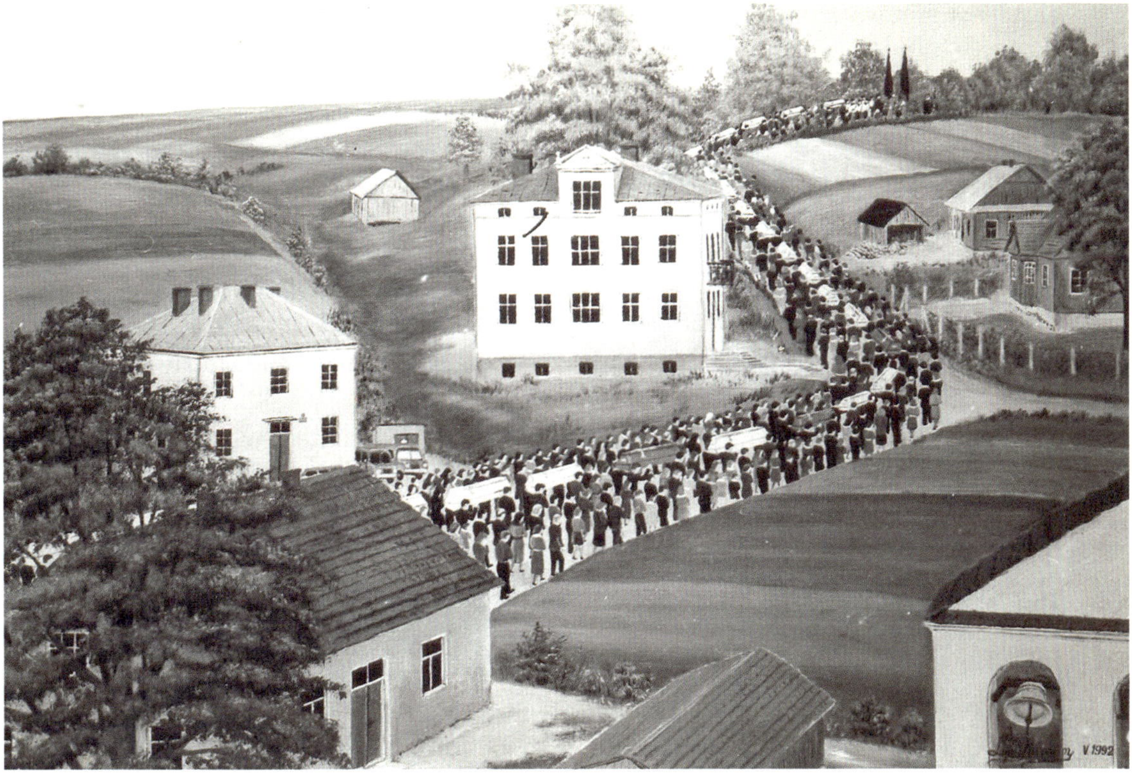

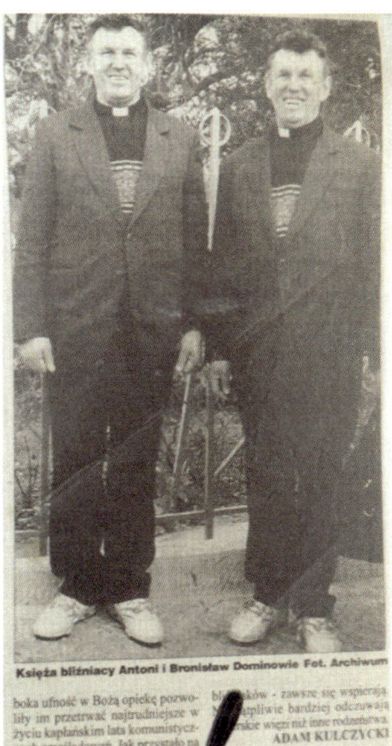

Księża bliźniacy Antoni i Bronisław Dominowie Fot. Archiwum

boka ufność w Bożą opiekę pozwoliły im przetrwać najtrudniejsze w życiu kapłańskim lata komunistycznych prześladowań. Jak przystało na

bli[illegible]ków - zawsze się wspierają. [illegible]atpliwie bardziej odczuwają [illegible]rskie więzi niż inne rodzeństwa.

ADAM KULCZYCKI

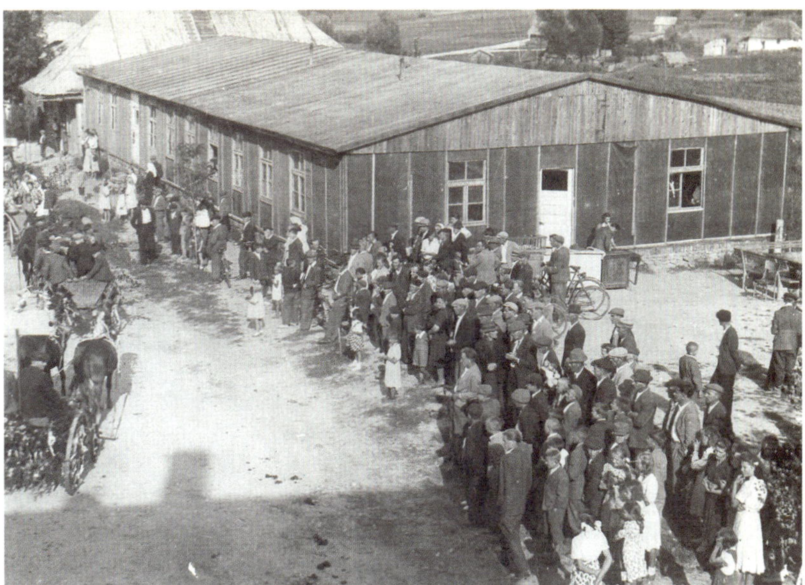

smallest plot was cultivated, because everybody was poor. The elongated strips of fields in the hill cracks are depicted in Lipa's painting like coloured ribbons, only a few of them larger than roads. The view is peaceful, nearly idyllic, yet one senses uneasiness.

The silhouettes of soldiers in 1915 are rigid, almost puppet-like. Those from 1939 also resemble figures whittled out of wood, but are more flexible. The events depicted in the paintings are frequently at odds with the order in the landscape. The irregular patterns of farmland, the arcs of the partitions, and the lack of right angles all bring forth some form of movement and mobility. Triangles and rhombuses move in relation to each other and overlap, producing a vertiginous effect. The painter was familiar with the rule of poetic effect, the rule of contrast that enabled him to convey doubt and ambiguity. He managed to fit questions into his merry-go-round of landscapes, placing significant and insignificant things next to each other: someone is dying in the foreground, while in the background someone is mowing grass.

Helena sang in the parish choir for ten years. In September she picks the last grapes from the sprouts withering on the stakes. She always laughs, whether she's talking about her age or illnesses, or about the good parish priest whom she served as a cook for 35 years. A photograph on the dresser shows a young Helena, who ran away twice when they brought her here to work. Helena hums Psalm 110 of the Vespers.

Twin priests dressed identically in a picture from an old newspaper. Father Bronisław lived in Szufnarowa, where he built a church in one night. His twin brother, Father Antoni, built the first illegal church of the Przemyśl Diocese in Babice at the request of Bishop Ignacy Tokarczuk. An exhibit of old household items Bronisław collected over the years, housed in a kitchen, contains a square table with a wooden suitcase placed on top. Next to the kitchen is a room with old school desks. Do the images converge because they come from the same landscape? Does life imitate art?

A **makeshift schoolhouse** housed in army barracks. I'm not sure whether the picture was taken by Roman Lipa or someone else. It was shot from one of the top floors of a building that still stands in the town square. The improvised sheds next to the market look rather unappealing in my contemporary photographs, but they become more expressive when I zoom in on the hills in the distance, in imitation of the painter. Again, a mix of significant and insignificant things: an important makeshift schoolhouse next door to an open-air market.

The faces on hundreds of Roman Lipa's first communion pictures are blurry and distant. Quite the opposite is true of his paintings: the faces are colourful, their expressions clear. The figures depicted at village celebrations have the faces of painted dolls, and in the painting *The Execution of 42 Jews in Wielopole Skrzyńskie on June 30, 1942*, their faces are terrified or rapt in prayer. The most terrified among them is the SS officer shooting the heads of the kneeling people. Lipa both painted and described this scene because he had learned of it through his neighbour, the head of the village at the time, whom the Nazis forced to participate in the execution. Lipa was the judge of his characters, as can be seen in the smooth, young, and indifferent look on the blue policeman's face. In the written chronicle of the event, the village head stood petrified, as he is portrayed in the painting. As a painter, Roman Lipa employed the tactic of combining contrastive elements, but he did not do so as a chronicler. Wishing to do justice to people, Lipa arranged his stories according to a hierarchy. This shift is an important issue in the reckoning of my archive.

The monument commemorates the 1955 fire of the schoolhouse, an event chronicled by Lipa. Housed in army barracks left behind by the Germans, the single classroom replaced the two destroyed at the front of the school, and traveling cinemas had just introduced highly flammable 35mm film. The reels were not allowed to be stored in the same room with the audience in Szufnarowa, so they were stocked in the projection room. One end of a film reel caught fire from a cigarette butt or a cable. The inebriated operator tried to put it out with his hands and shoes, and when that failed, the crew escaped through the window and drove off. Dozens of spectators died, most of them children, along with people attempting to rescue them. The remains of those who could not be identified were trucked out to the cemetery and buried in one grave. The bodies of those who had not yet been identified by their families were taken to the morgue on the orders of the government and the event was hastily covered up, writes Lipa. A few years ago a performance of the oratorio *From Beneath the Cross of the Burned* was held in Wielopole. The piece was composed by a local musician, choirmaster, and organ player.

Though a ritual commemorating the terrible event was held, something still remains. I would like to uncover the missing part of the picture. Roman

Lipa described the fire in extraordinary detail. His description has survived. Regarding the description of my archive, however, it does not provide a satisfactory answer, but merely poses new questions for me. Some of them were also posed by Tadeusz Kantor, who wrote about the "storehouses" and "catalogues" of our memory, full of insignificant details and detritus that persist motionless, as clear as a film negative. Roman Lipa apparently wanted to prevent such motionlessness. The unpublished state of his writings reduces his hope of success. Thus there is no collective memory, but merely a chaotic assembly of individual memories competing with each other; there are protective barriers at work.

the cinema

Lipa arrived too late. He was a firefighter who failed to save children from the flames and a photographer who failed to take pictures of the funeral. He later painted the procession. All of this lends an internal motion to his testimony.

"[…] I was the only participant of the funeral who owned a camera. As soon as I attempted to take my first picture of the procession of four caskets approaching the church gates from the market square, three men came up to me and introduced themselves as secret police officers. They forbade me to take pictures of the public gathering under penalty of law […]. I was surrounded by the police and secret police officers throughout the whole funeral, and was not even allowed to take my camera out at the cemetery. My great desire was to take a shot of the several hundred-meter-long procession of white caskets from a distance. It would have been a souvenir documenting the tragic event. My police and secret police escort followed my every move. […] If I had foreseen such behaviour on the part of the security services, I would have prepared for the circumstances and taken such a picture from the church attic […]."

Graeme Miller

IMMEMORIAL

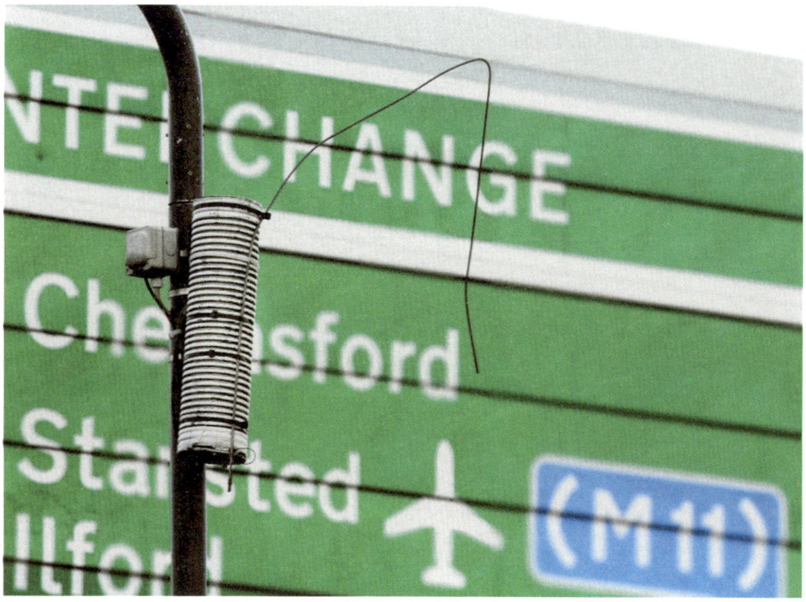

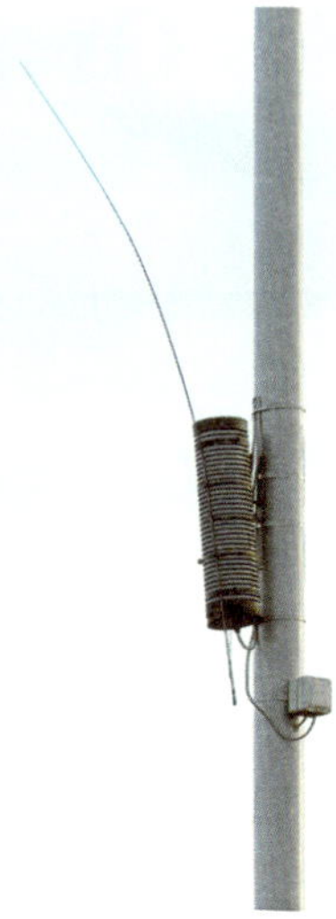

I have come back to Hackney Marshes to check how many transmitters of *Linked* are still working. The work has run now for 11 years. I take a seat in the nearly empty Velodrome that has appeared next to the site of the former Spooky Lady pub, one of my sites.

A dozen men are in quiet elliptical orbit swooping from far away to suddenly near. Two women are using their phones to photograph individual cyclists as they pass. It is the £30 Taster session given, I guess, as a gift. The cyclists are in fixed formation and so, to each other they are more or less still. Likewise at the fairground the tin car I am in and the tin train ahead of me are in constant range and focus unlike the perimeter that is a blurred frieze in which my parents' blurred smile and blurred wave appear regularly. They are clocking my laps: my noon and midnight. My constant. Their job: my witness. The blur hides the complex emotions I later feel watching my own child on such a ride, clocking his progress, but sensing a portent of separation, bolted against the centrifugal force of his own highway. Buying a ride then is a ticket to a little performance about time. An onlooked ride is a ritual of passing. One acts the flow while the other stands still against it—a stick in the stream.

The transmitters of *Linked* were put up in 2003. Each one is encoded with the voices of former residents who speak of spaces—500 buildings that include the house I myself lived in for 10 years. They were demolished to build the M11 Link Road motorway. The voices speak of their own whereabouts into their own whereabouts where pools of analogue broadcast can be heard with a receiver. They speak into a radically changed landscape, describing wallpaper into the six lanes of urban motorway. You have to *be there* to listen and in this way the work is about space and site. Yet listening is a real-time act making the work equally about time and its progress. As it progresses from its start in 2003, the more the work speaks of time. Each antenna loops the same unchanging eight minutes of audio. An eddy. A governor. A cog. These antennae mark their visitation. Sticks in the stream.

The work placed its launch at the hinge of its 200-year time frame. It reaches back to the last period of rapid top-down change when the buildings traumatically demolished in 1994 were traumatically constructed on green fields in 1894. It holds scenes a century old (family memory can reach 150 years in one 80-year-old's retelling of a scene from her grandparent's childhood). I was told by Simon Beer, who designed the transmitters, that their ultra-stable chips will bear those descriptions 100 years forwards. That journey has discernably begun to fill the progress bar.

The audio mixes up time in an impersonation of the layered nature of narrative at each site. It is impressionistic and slightly vertiginous, consisting of fragments rather than stories. To avoid the exile of the past tense and the tone of rehearsed storytelling, speakers were asked to recall in the present tense. Ongoing moments are spoken (and heard)—*ongoingly* bringing two strands of the present together. The pedestrian listener completes the circuit by filling the gaps with their own narrative. They activate the work by staying still for a few minutes. Their present is their gift. Present. Presence. Present. The listener is invited into a temporal flow that is a kind of circulating blur in which they, in real time, are the marker of the onrush. Noon and Midnight. They move the hinge forwards.

The shutter on the camera phone is quite slow in low light, so the passing rider dissolves in coloured stripes into their own trajectory. If you turn the camera to follow the rider they come clear but the background blurs. It is a negotiation. The familiarity of the mid-field becomes unfamiliar with distance and proximity. Different distances and different speeds make this a territory hard for the eye to steer through. You have to navigate the blur with imagination, perceive through the fog with the radar of the heart.

In Leyton I observed at first hand the effect of one side of a two-sided street being demolished. It is suddenly clear they have been holding each other in place, accounting for each other all these years. With one side gone the other just seems to leak its narrative juices. *Linked* is a skeletal structure whose spine draws in witnesses to repair the narrative tissue of its location. It works by being heard. Walking and listening creates new flesh. Yet the work exists mostly unheeded. Mostly it is not-listened-to and un-walked. Re-walking this route from the Olympic Park to Redbridge, I am amazed by the fact that most transmitters are still going strong. I attribute them with human characteristics in their loyal endurance and the sheer bravery of their disregard for attention. They build a secret world. As your receiver crackles into life you can sense this autonomy. As the voices fade you get a hint of their continued presence at your parting. They are transmitting now and to date have done so three-quarter of a million times. The visitor marks the dial of their looping. Their looping marks time's highway.

Checking the transmitter at the south end of Grove Green Road I happen to catch my own voice. I am describing glass flying down the hallway as police smash down my front door. We are having breakfast. Gabriel my son is there. I leave this moment to loop, dazed by complexity. The work is not about preserving memories, which , even at a neural level, are not things, but pathways. I walk on with a viral

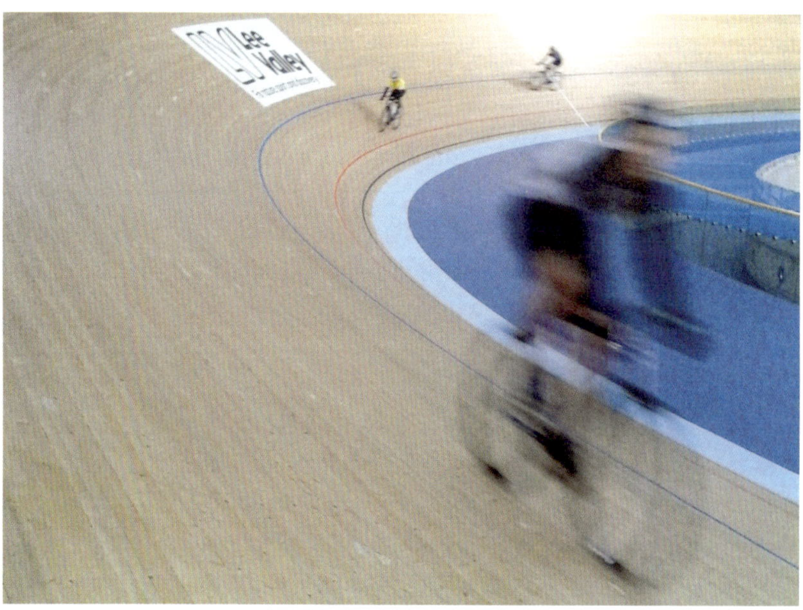

rebirth of my own experience that might well be reborn in someone else's neural and pedestrian pathways. They will be walked away, forgotten, mis-remembered, eroded.

Time has been busy working on the landscape around. What is surprising is how much remains the same. Time has also been busy on the work about Time. A transmitter was knocked down by a lorry, then lost. Outside the Velodrome another had to be taken down to dodge the corporate onrush of the Olympic Park. Another one or two need fixing. Water gets in. These are hints of the work's eventual demise. It has begun a trajectory of increasing privacy that will end with the last word of the final broadcast of the last transmitter. It will be a funnelled process I myself will leave. Simon Beer died this year, Gabriel too during the Olympics that themselves came and went. Motion blur. Emotion blur.

I have had the back off the watch of this work. The watchmaker's head spins at the complexity of cogs. Emanations of the end raise the strange question of conservation. How to choreograph demise? The answer, for the time being, is to fix a few things in this contraption while letting its own absence crash into itself. This "semi-permanent" artwork is already in discussion with its own semi-permanence. I navigate the blurring movement increasingly with the heart aware that this, my glimpse at this work in late 2014 and this, its written account and this, your reading, along with each future re-reading, retelling, re-printing, and remembering added to all those of the past are its mechanism.

Heidi & Rolf Abderhalden / Mapa Teatro

TESTIGOS

WITNESSES

In the poietical cartography of Mapa Teatro (Bogotá, Colombia), *Testigo de las ruinas* (Witness to the ruins, 2002–2012) is one of the most significant poetic-political gestures. Not only because of the *extensive* nature of Mapa's work and its creative processes (in time and space) and because of the *intensity* of its praxis (involving the development of an "experimental temporary community" and a "laboratory of social imagination" in a Bogotá neighbourhood destined to be torn down), but also due to the singular and paradoxical tension between its *acts* (multiple deployments of one and the same event) and its *formal acts* (the archive's diversity of shapes and folds).

Antanas Mockus is sitting alone, in silence, on a corner of an old couch, under the dim light of a lamp that is leaning beside him. He is wearing a grey suit and a tie, indigo blue. The man who ruled the capital of Colombia, from 1995 to 1997 and from 2001 to 2003, watches the images projected in front of him on a green translucent mesh that divides the space. Facing him, on the other side of the mesh-screen, a heterogeneous audience watches the same images and hears the sounds and the voices that go with them. Amid the two groups, on the threshold of this dispositif, we, Heidi and Rolf Abderhalden, responsible for this encounter, observe the one and the others observing: witnesses of witnesses. Between official history and collective fictions, the mythical tale and local mythologies: unaffective institutional documents face-to-face with personal archives laden with affects.

We are in the San Francisco Museum of Modern Art (SFMOMA) on December 11, 2012, ten years after Mapa Teatro's first action performed in El Cartucho. The images and sounds projected today show fragments of the demolition process of the Santa Inés neighbourhood, known as El Cartucho, in Bogotá: images that we recorded ourselves, or found in different archives, from 2002 to 2005. All images are part of the various artistic actions that we realized from 2002 to 2012 around one of the most ambitious "urban renewal" projects in Bogotá and, concerning which, we wanted to be *witnesses* and at the same time *cartographers*, collectively.

The immemorial childhood image of El Cartucho that I bear on my body, the place of our childhood mythologies, both personal and collective, is that of a man covered in grease, the blackened skin beneath a scrap of a blanket. The man carries a box of matches in his hand and something I do not recognize between his lips. The man walks barefoot, his manhood protruding. I wait for my mother in the car, parked right on the street. I see the man through the glass. The man sees me. I lower my head. The man approaches. I close my eyes. Night falls. Forty years later, with the same childish fear, I walk after him through the rubble and the remaining streets in El Cartucho. Jairo-*Charon*, in person, guides us to the bottom circle of hell to meet and gather together fifteen *Prometheuses*, men and women, of different ages, occupations and backgrounds, as witnesses and *living archives* of the last episode of the history of this mythical, foundational place. All of them have accepted Mapa's invitation to share with us the desire to *witness/chart* its memory.

It is in this *virtual* field, at the city limits, that Mapa Teatro were to perform its first actions: *Prometeo I Acto* (2002), *Prometeo II Acto* (2003), and *Re/corridos* (2003). This same year, prior to the demolition of the last Cartucho house where she lived, we had the opportunity to meet Juana Ramírez, a woman who resisted leaving the ruins where she still slept and worked, selling *arepas* (tortillas made of corn) and hot chocolate in the midst of a devastated landscape. The account of her life in the Santa Inés-El Cartucho neighbourhood became, after a fourth and final site-specific action, *La Limpieza de los establos de Augías* (Cleaning of the Augean Stables, 2004) and led to the inauguration of the "Third Millennium Park," the backbone of a "final" action, *Testigo de las ruinas* (Witness to the Ruins, 2005): the name given to the performance dispositif that gathers together the series of actions developed over ten years.

In 2006, *Witness to the Ruins* underwent a major transformation by virtue of the context where it was shown—a keynote lecture at an international conference on Latin American cinema at the University of Cambridge—a new dispositif that allowed us to problematize and re-activate our notion of archive outside the "original" work. One of us would take the role of speaker in a keynote speech where, because of the conditions and the presentation format, he or she would suddenly become part of the archive material.

Years later, in 2011 in New York, in order to commemorate the tenth anniversary of 9/11, Columbia University invited Mapa Teatro to participate in an academic event called *Injured Cities*, with the presentation of a lecture-performance of *Testigo de las ruinas*. This format, a hybrid of conference and performative act, led us to install on the Miller Theater stage some vestiges of the original staging of *Testigo de las Ruinas*. Instead of a white screen, typical of traditional academic conferences, we opted for a translucent green mesh, such as those used in Colombia for construction work in public spaces, and projected onto it the images of the five actions that had been performed until then. Behind this mesh we mounted low lights that would allow the two "speaker-performers" (Heidi and Rolf Abderhalden) to appear and disappear like ghosts of the same image at different times of the presentation. From there, both of us read and discussed the images and testimonials projected—the visual and sound archive of the work—re-activating the archive once again in a new *happening*, a sort of sixth *montage* of this set of actions.

In 2012, Antanas Mockus is taking part, for the first time with us, in a new experiment of this lecture performance, presented as part of a Marathon Camp in Graz (Austria) on art and politics under the title *Truth is Concrete*, a meeting to which he was also invited for other lectures and interviews. Ten years after his mandate in Bogotá City Hall, the former mayor accepts the experiment by expressing, *live* and out loud in front of the images projected before him, the deeply felt impressions and reflections awoken in him by an archive of which he is part, in a kind of dialogue with the *ghosts*: his own as mayor and citizen, the city's as a collective subject.

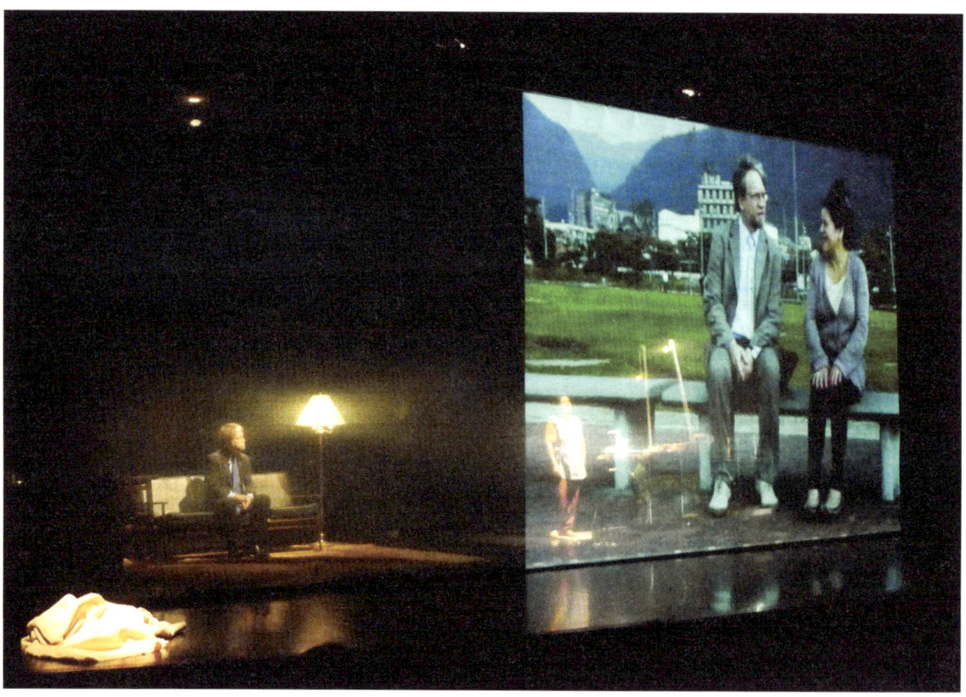

In San Francisco, the man, the philosopher, the *artist*, is positioned beside the stage next to Juana Ramírez. In this *theatre of memory* the former mayor and the last inhabitant of El Cartucho meet for the first time since then to close, or perhaps *open*, an archive that is embodied, thus bringing full circle a poetic-political experience that had been born ten years earlier and has been re-activated again and again: in the images they watch of the past the ruler, firm in his decision, oversees the demolition, while the woman resists from fear of not being able to live outside that place; a decade later, on stage, she can finally accept how the changes were beneficial for her, while he sadly recognizes how arbitrary the exercise of power is. We have all now become the object of observation: they who observe, affected, and we who observe them with our own affects.

The archive is the *artwork*; the *artwork* is the *archive*.

canecapovolto & Elisa Abela

CONDOMINIO

CONDOMINIUM

THE HERMIT

(based on an idea by Caterina Devi)

"Search your memory, independent women and men, for the figure and name of a patron, an acquaintance, a client, a relative, a friend who lives in a place less dangerous than yours. Ask this person for information and advice. Someone will finally show you a hut, a cabin, a shed whose ramshackle structure will make you feel safe."

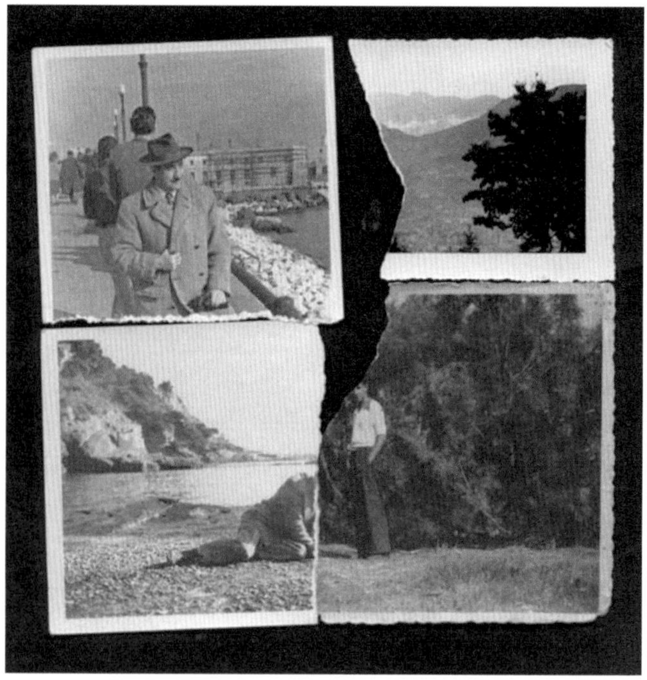

A condominium is a type of housing community defined in legal terms.
We can speak of a condominium when, in a building consisting of a number of apartments, there are tenants who are exclusive owners of a part of the aforesaid building; the same tenants are also co-owners of the common spaces in the building.
More generally, the term refers to any building that is divided into apartments.

The operation called *The Hermit* was born out of an intuition of the artist Caterina Devi. The idea was to slip a number of messages composed in the form of collage by Elisa Abela into the mailboxes of apartment blocks in Rome, Catania, and Palermo. Concurrently, the operator called canecapovolto made seven numbered video messages and posted them on the Internet.

A STOLEN CONVERSATION

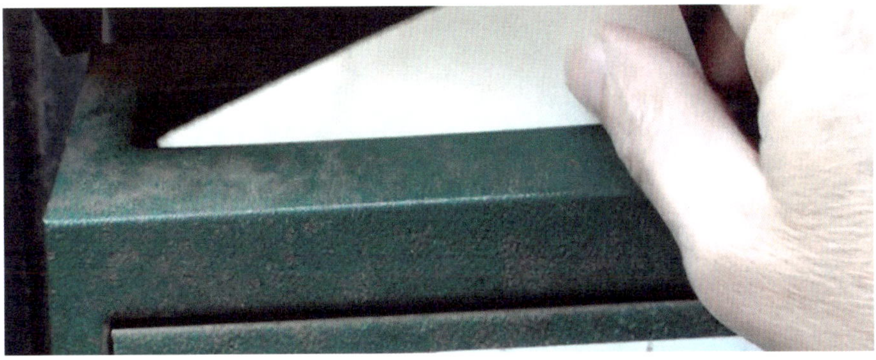

Q: It must have been the tenant on the fifth floor.
R: Maybe. Have you heard any noises?
Q: Yes ...early in the morning!
R: Then it surely was the tenant on the fifth floor.

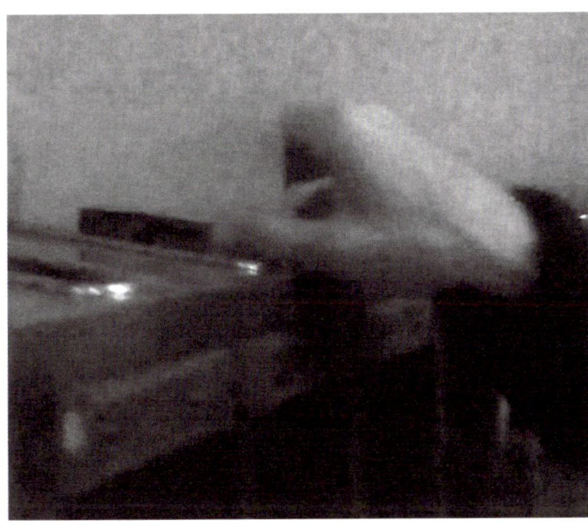

Advertising is meant to reach, at random, the largest number of people.
The end result is beyond anyone's guess.
On the contrary, the aim of the Hermit is to address the smallest number of people.
No more than two in each condominium.

Q: Can you feel the smell coming from behind his door?
R: Sure. Smell of alcohol.
Q: If one worries too much about cleaning, something fishy must be going on.
R: Sure.
Q: He is gone now.

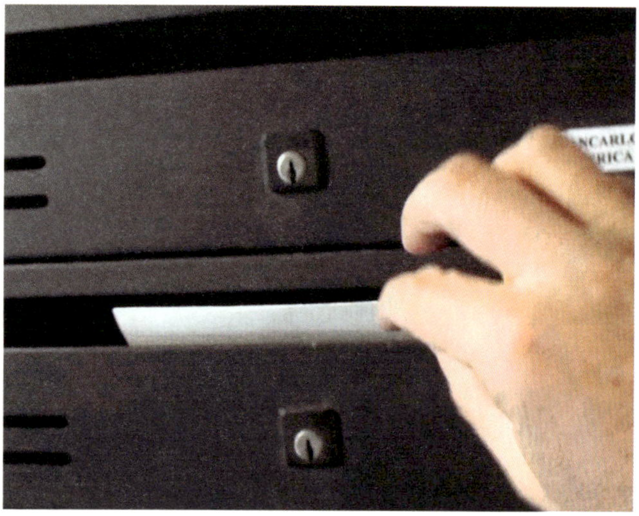

R: *They paid me a visit today but I wasn't in.*
Q: *I was.*

The message of the circular letter reads:
"I paid you a visit today but you weren't in."

"The Hermit does not boast any erudite ambitions. Although his project has been conceived and developed as a scientific project, it has no intention of replacing or pre-empting the laws and regulations of the community.

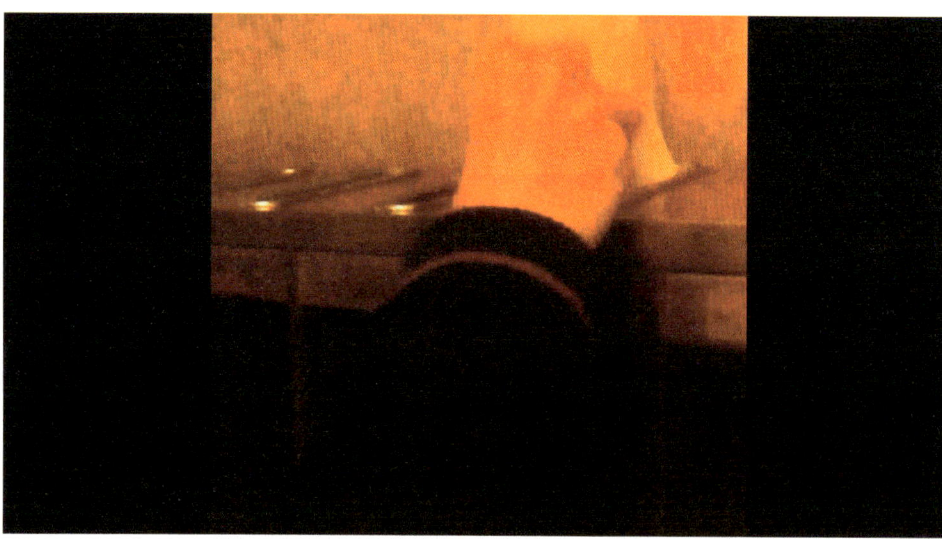

The project is only meant to suggest to citizens what independent measures they can take to protect themselves and their family against the hidden dangers lurking behind the apparent safety of living in a condominium, or generally speaking behind any large-scale mass operation."

"Having done that, the Hermit's mission will be considered accomplished."

There are always interpersonal dynamics remaining dangerously inert and unstable for years.
This is exactly what we are ardently pinning our hopes on.
Five or six circular letters in each district will be sufficient; the cold winterly wind will do the rest. Would you rather leave propaganda in the hands of priests and fanatics only?
That would be an unforgivable mistake.

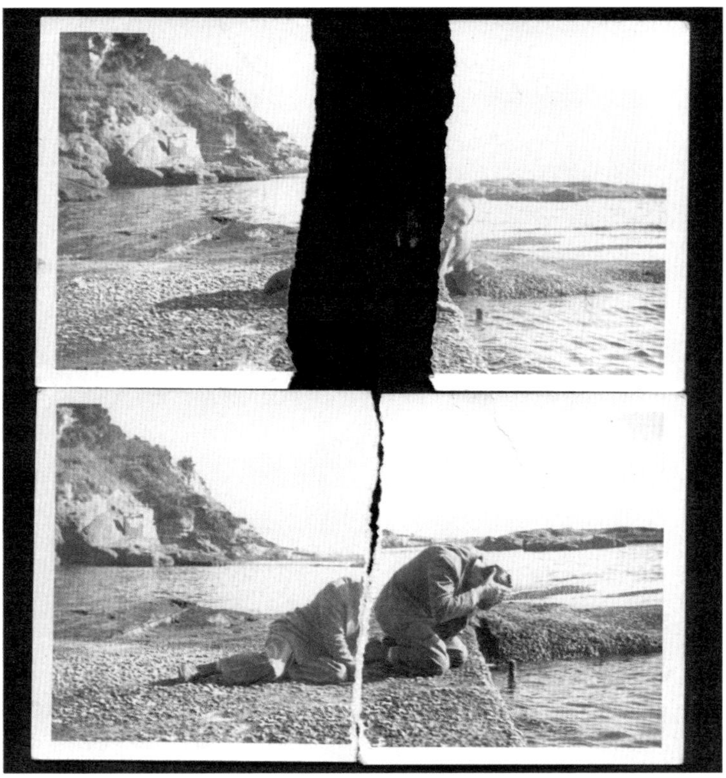

One thing is for sure: the end result is beyond anyone's guess.
Anyway, I paid you a visit today but you weren't in.

Paola Di Cori

VOLVER

RETURN

Volver... con la frente marchita,
las nieves del tiempo platearon mi sien

(To return, with my forehead all wrinkled,
my temples turned silver by time's falling snow...)

('Volver', music by Carlos Gardel, 1935, lyrics by Alfredo Le Pera)

The last time I was in Buenos Aires, a few years ago, I rented a small apartment, 100 metres away from the house I used to live in from the late 1940s until 1962; in a quiet street, in the poorer part of the district known as "Palermo viejo" (the one of Evaristo Carriego, to be clear), not to be confused with "Palermo chico," an area of embassies and the rich bourgeoisie. Every day in August, which was cold and rainy as Argentinian winters have now become, I would walk through the district just to be able to pass in front of a modest three-storey house squeezed in between two tall residential buildings, which had been built later. I would stop for a while to look at the white facade, as if waiting for something to happen (I didn't know what), then continue my walk.

On previous occasions, I never forgot to walk past the house of my childhood at least once; if I did forget, I felt a bit guilty after my return to Italy. Like someone who finally sets off on a spiritual pilgrimage or plans a visit to an art gallery to see an exhibition, but once she is there, forgets to go into the church or the museum, and only then realizing that her destination was meant to be different. As a matter of fact, I'd always had plenty of time, so I must have intentionally avoided to walk past my home, after all.

The home was the problem. Or rather its façade. Especially the balcony on the second floor, long and narrow. Extremely sombre, even in summer. There I used to be locked out, as a punishment, when I was misbehaving, like that traumatic afternoon—I was three at that time—which I spent crying desperately, unable to get back into the apartment until evening. I hated this place also because it was protected with robust metal bars fixed on top of a double railing made of black iron to prevent accidents which could happen to children. Seen out of the window of my room, the only one in the small apartment which had two French windows, the bars made an unpleasant, prison-like impression. Whether outside or inside the apartment I could never get rid of a sense of living in seclusion.

In order to better understand this feeling, during my last journey I finally decided to confront this bleak balcony by daily systematic surveillance. I would stop on the other side of the street right in front of the main entrance framed by dark marble tiles and bearing a white metal plate with an enamelled number in the upper left corner. Both wings of the wooden doors, once kept open, were now closed. I would stand there, quite still, gazing at the modest façade as if I was waiting for something to happen that could stand as a testimony to my encounter and to my firm decision to face up to the potential threats of the old balcony. But nothing ever happened: the building was silent and after some time I would walk away. And so it went on for four weeks.

I felt as the hero of *El comun olvido*, a novel by Sylvia Molloy, who has lived in New York for years but often comes back to Buenos Aires and there he walks through the city, lost and confused. In the city, which used to be so close to him and so hospitable, he finds only dispersed fragments; a lot of its areas are now empty and mysterious. He recognizes a sign board of some shop, a new tenement house which has now replaced a laundry; but the whole of it seems alien and unclear to him. Probably, the street, too, with my old house and its fateful balcony wanted to tell me with their peace and quiet that, at the end of the day, there was nothing to look for.

Back in Italy, I developed a roll of film and suddenly four pictures of the famous façade appeared. I thought I would try once more. I chose one photo in which the building and the balcony could be seen quite clearly and put it on a side shelf in the living room so that I could decide whether to look at the picture or avoid it, depending on the moment. Sometimes I would stop to give it a distracted glance. Months and finally a year passed. The photo was silent. Sometimes I would think maybe the time had come to put it away. But where? I wasn't sure which place would be most appropriate for the picture. Certainly, I didn't want to risk losing it in one of the numerous drawers, cluttered with business cards, index cards, medical prescriptions, letters, paper clips, bank statements. Maybe I should put it in a book? Hiding the picture made me really anxious, but keeping the photo on the shelf was an equally disturbing option. Because of its poor quality I was not inclined to mount it in a frame, yet I was also alarmed by the prospect of interfering with its simple condition as a 5×7" photo lying vulnerable on a shelf. The idea to set it upright was unacceptable because I might come across it unexpectedly. However, such an inflexible alternative had to be broken; this obstinate and annoying confrontation had to be sidestepped.

I began by transferring the picture onto my computer desktop. The photo was a printout of a negative, which I had taken with an old camera. So I had to go to the photo lab round the corner and ask if they could transfer it onto a pen drive since only then I could save it as a Word file. The outcome would by no means be perfect because of the poor quality of the original, but my decision was decisive for other reasons.

First of all, this ruse took me "away from the street." I was no longer standing in the open air, in the cold, looking up to the second floor. I would be able to open and close the file that showed the house while sitting comfortably at my desk; I could study it closely and from a distance, contrast the different angles from which the photos were taken and compare them by laying one picture on top of another. Although the balcony itself did not tell me much, the pictures did. I noticed some details which I had overlooked when standing in front of the house, staring at it fully immersed in the old drama of my childhood. I had not noticed before the two sculpted masks placed above the window nor the fact that the balcony on the third floor was different from the other two. While it lacked the curved shape which made the two balconies downstairs more refined, it had a double line of balusters opening in the middle; at any rate, an atrocious building which was added later ended up spoiling the overall look of the house.

There was nothing else to do but leave the house as it was in those unappealing photos, at which I looked now with placid resignation: grey, taciturn, remote.

Rome, 12 December 2014, on my 68th birthday

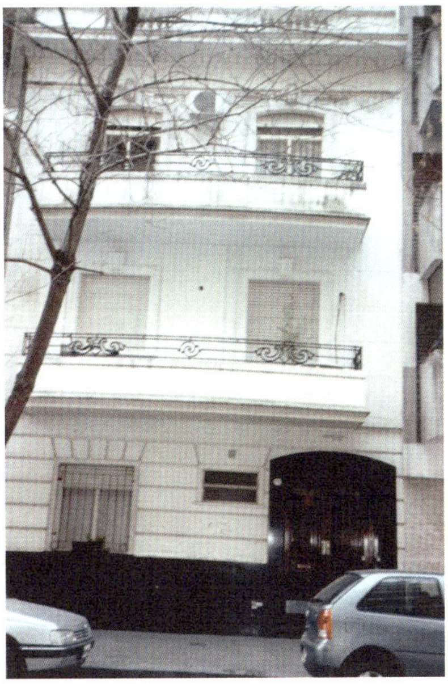

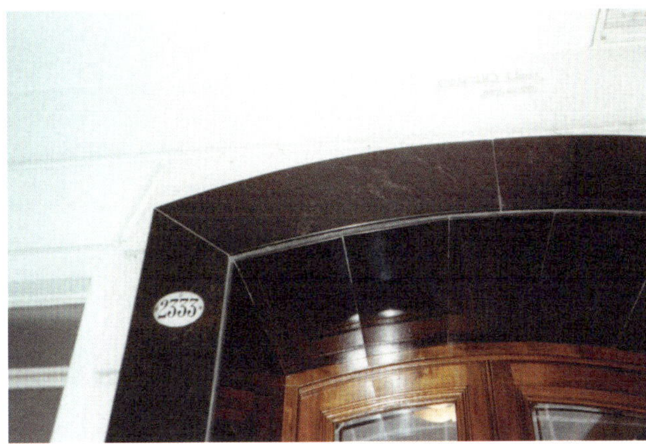

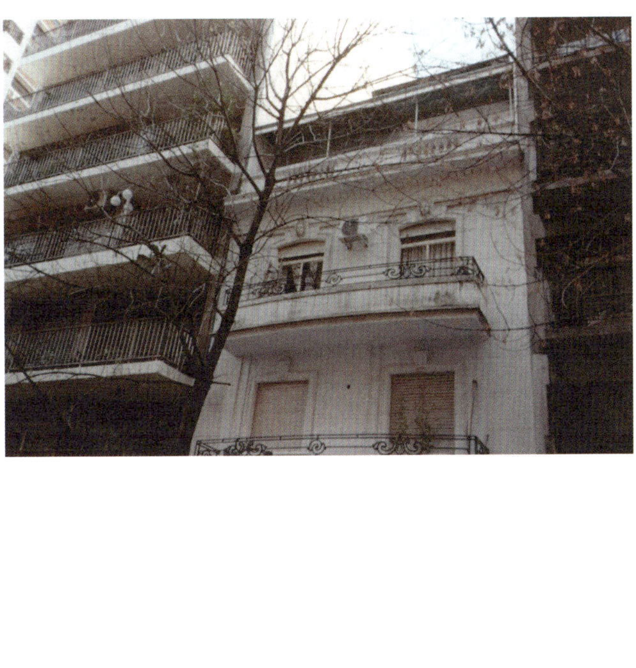

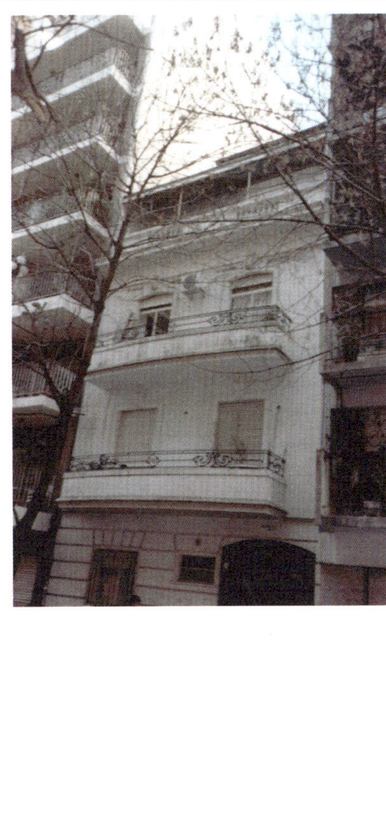

Joe Kelleher

UNANSWERED

I have been able to find three of the photos online. The rest, nearly two years after the event, will have to be from memory. But here is what I have found. The "merch girl" in professional rock-and-roll photographer Joe Stevens' black-and-white image looks like she has something on her mind. The lit cigarette held between two fingers of her right hand appears forgotten about. The same goes for the sheet of torn corrugated cardboard hanging from a string around her neck, on which are pinned the rosettes she is selling: pieces of crimped ribbon in a range of shades, each rosette displaying a picture of *Aladdin Sane*-era David Bowie with a stapled paper caption: "DAVID BOWIE IS GREAT." I am guessing that is not official merchandise. The rosette on her own chest is pinned on sideways. She herself is staring out of the frame, lost in a thought. I don't imagine she is thinking about David Bowie at that moment, but who is to say now.

Other images from this particular archive are by amateur photographers, fan photos taken by people who were there for the shows. That may be the case with the one in colour of the four young women, late teens or early twenties, long-haired (centre partings each one), standing close together, a group of friends I'm guessing, lined up and showing off their—this time—official merchandise. They hold up for the camera David Bowie 1973 tour programmes with that same image (the star is bare-shouldered, eyes closed, orange haired, made up with the iconic red and blue lightning-flash across his forehead and right eye and cheek) from the *Aladdin Sane* album cover. Three of the women are sporting the same lightning-flash on their own faces. One of them—the only one who is making eye contact with the camera—is grinning with delight.

The third photo is from the same time but addresses a different topic and occasion. A black-and-white press photograph: a city street, terraced houses blurring into the distance along the right-hand side of the image. In the middle ground the hulk of a taxi cab, unoccupied, driven half-way up onto the pavement, where it should not be, its front fender hanging off, a lighter patch on the road beside the car that might be broken glass. In the deep background, at the end of the street, two plumes of black smoke rise between the buildings. In the foreground, the only sharply focused detail in the picture, a young face, helmeted with the visor up, peers out from behind an obstacle, the barrel of an army rifle poking out beside the face. The face itself—so very young—could be that of a boy or a girl. I am presuming the former, but from the features alone—the eyes, the lips, the expression—you wouldn't necessarily know.

Where to start with the archive? Meaning here by "archive" a number of materials, utterances, expressions, recordings, images (in this case it happens to be photographic images, visual traces of events), gathered and arranged for someone, anyone—others, oneself—to consult and converse with, for the sake of a memory or a counter-memory, so that something may be known, known again, known otherwise. So that knowledge may be worked up. Where does the knowing start? This archive, as it happens, is accompanied by a map so maybe we should have started there, although the map—or we might think of it rather as a sort of catalogue—only tells us so much. It is large, though, filling almost an entire wall, and consisting of a silhouette of the British Isles in thin black outline. The outline is crossed by a network of even thinner red lines, occasionally stretching into the areas of Wales and Scotland, but mostly concentrated around England. There are no red lines on the outline of the Irish land-mass. The map interrupts the display of photographs, which are otherwise arranged in a single, regularly spaced strip at eye level around the walls of the gallery. The photos are of a scale that means you have to go up close, you have to follow them round, to see what they have to show. What they show turns out to be pictures from David Bowie's 18-month 1972–73 tour of the United Kingdom to promote the *Ziggy Stardust and the Spiders from Mars* and *Aladdin Sane* albums (the itinerary of which is marked out by those red lines criss-crossing England, Scotland Wales), intercut with press images that document the significant social upheaval taking place across Britain and Ireland at that time, including protests against large-scale industrial lay-offs and above all the civil rights demonstrations and bombings that made up the early and intense period of the Northern Irish Troubles. Bowie's tour, which started the day before the Bloody Sunday violence in Derry when a number of civil rights demonstrators were shot and killed by British army soldiers, never made it to Northern Ireland.

I say archive, although what I am talking about in fact is an artwork that involves what Hal Foster characterized in an essay of the same title as an "archival impulse." A ready-organized counter-memory, so to speak. Affects and associations already sign-posted and road-tested by someone who got to the material first and gave it a shape and who is sending us now, well, what shall we call it?, a message, a bulletin, a sort of interim report on their findings? Here, the commissioning of the map (which was made by Scott King) and the sourcing and arranging of the photographs together make up a piece by artist Jeremy Deller. The piece was called "Bevan tried to change the nation," and itself made up one part of Deller's exhibition *English Magic* for the British Pavilion at the 2013 Venice Biennale.

For want of space I won't say anything more, at least not directly, about *English Magic*, although I would like to stay just a little longer with "Bevan tried to change the nation," the title of which is a line from Bowie's song "Star" on the *Ziggy Stardust* album, and which references the post-war Labour politician Aneurin Bevan who was the architect of Britain's National Health Service, who is set alongside Tony who "went to fight in Belfast" and Rudi who "stayed at home to starve" and Sonny who "wants to turn the world," all of whom counterpoint the escapist rock star dreams of the song's persona. What the photographs, brought together in this way, seem to say and to show is how small some of the differences might appear to be between one expression of the nation's dreaming and another, how insignificant the distances between the dreamers. The young people on the civil rights marches and those at the rock concert look like they could be the same people. In some of the images, it is not even clear at once whether this is a record of a rock concert or a demo, a pop culture document, or a political culture document. Even the Starman himself, the one on stage on the other side of the sound monitors, whose face is on the album covers and the cheap rosettes, inches away from the ones who are reaching out towards him, the spangle suit looking itchy enough, guitarist Mick Ronson grinning and preening at his side, everyone there in that converted cinema or college hall, or wherever it is they are sweating the same sweat, enveloped by the same no-longer-audible noise, even he doesn't look so strange or faraway as we might have imagined or remembered him, he no more than any. As if by some sort of magic of the archive, they could all be there at once, any of the kids in all of the photos, from all points of the map. And be there with each other in all their lucidity; where, to borrow a formulation from the philosopher Paul Ricoeur, "carefree memory" is at work "on the horizon of concerned memory, the soul common to memory that forgets and does not forget."

And how might such magic be invoked? Perhaps by leaving the archival message, bulletin, or report unanswered, unread after all. Which is not to say ignored or unattended, but rather unread in the way we might mark an email message as "unread" having already looked at it and knowing we will need to return to it. Knowing there is still something to do. Knowing that the images—and much else beside—have not done with us yet either.

Tina Campt

STASIS

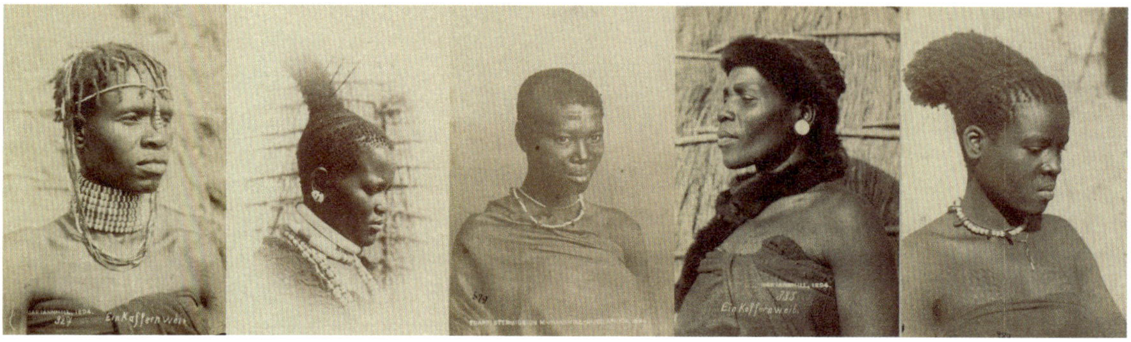

The native's muscles are always tensed. You can't say that he is terrorized, or even apprehensive. He is in fact ready at a moment's notice to exchange the role of the quarry for that of the hunter.

(Frantz Fanon, *Wretched of the Earth*, 1963)

T This entry begins and ends with two confessional moments. Confession #1: These images vex me. They are photographs that affect me and images in which I see a multitude of things. I'm conflicted by the beauty I see in them, and perplexed by the quiet introspection they so hauntingly depict. I see images of black women with dignity and stature. I see regal and penetrating gazes downcast, looking outward, or focused on the camera. Yet viewed in their historical and institutional context, they witness a transliteration of beauty into racialized cultural categories and confront us with a vulnerability that also frames each of these women's photographic presentation. In and around their strength and vulnerability, I see, as well, what most viewers take for granted: their stillness.

But what appears to be motionlessness is, in fact, an effortful placement. Darieck Scott describes this tension as an arrested activity held back in restraint—the tensions of a new consciousness "that readies itself to direct the body in activity" as a "reservoir of resistance to the colonizer's acts of subjugation and enslavement." While I agree with Scott's description, I describe it with a different vocabulary. I call it *stasis*. What changes in our apprehension of images of the colonized and dispossessed when we look beyond "passive" immobility and engage them through the lens of stasis?

sta•sis:

1. *an act or condition of standing or stopping;*
2. *an effortful practice of achieving balance or equilibrium among various forces.*

These images require us to *see* stasis, and to see it as a form of motion held in tension and suspension. They require us to recognize the forms of muscular tension imaged in them as a *performance of stillness* that is an active attempt to arrest both physical and affective motion, which never attains the complete cessation of either.

Each of these photos are numbered, dated, and stamped: *"Mariannhill-Süd-Afrika 1894."* But one word is missing in several of these images: *Trappistenmission*—Trappist Mission. Brought to the Eastern Cape in 1880, the Trappists were recruited to South Africa to build model farms intended to convert Africans to Christianity by educating them in the Christian faith and efficient farming methods. The Mariannhill Mission was established in 1882 in Pinetown, near Durban, in what is currently KwaZulu-Natal. One of the many workshops built as part of the brothers' efforts to be an autonomous, self-sustaining enterprise of Christian conversion in the colony was a photography studio, where at least two of the brothers served as its official photographers, documenting daily life in the mission and among the native communities in and around it through portraits and other photographic depictions of their inhabitants. While many of these images were published in the mission's periodicals and newsletters, numerous others were sent to financial benefactors, or sold as scientific evidence to amateur and professional collectors and ethnographic museums.

The photographs of these five women clearly belong to the group of images that circulated in the traffic between the mission, the collector, and the museum. They are portraits, some even *cartes de visite*—albeit ones accompanied by ethnographic attributions on their opposite sides. These attributions do not identify these women by name; they label them instead as "Kaffervrouw," "Kaffernweib," or "Itombi Mädchen." They annotate them according to jewellery, headdress, hairstyle, and skin markings, thus appropriating their subjects' chosen adornments of self-fashioning as references to their place in an ethnographic catalogue. Their annotations translate these striking figures into visual categories that reproduce them as subjugated people.

But the affects of these photos are different. They are atmospheric and aestheticized, almost beatific representations of aura and inwardness. They aestheticize their black subjects into a temporal elsewhere outside of history. This aesthetic was neither benign nor romantic. The depiction of timeless Africans frozen in an unspoiled wilderness was deployed to invoke an idyllic image of authentic native culture that required "separation" and "protection." Such depictions were the visual instantiation of the central arguments used to justify the Native Land Act of 1913, which displaced thousands of black South Africans from their land, and laid the ideological groundwork for racial restructuring and segregation that became the backbone of Apartheid rule.

Engaging these women as tensely embodied, muscular subjects in stasis complicates the meaning of self-fashioning. The forms of stasis they capture do not necessarily render them either inherent enactments of resistance or thoroughly abject supplicants. Rather, it poses a more radical and potentially less satisfying question: what might we gain by uncoupling the notion of *self-fashioning* from the concept of *agency*? What I'm suggesting is that the concept of stasis helps us to see these images as complex articulations of self that refuse both easy categorization and oppositional understandings of agency versus subjection. They are photos that instantiate what Scott, reprising Fanon, describes as "powerfulness in debility." The muscular tension they depict remind us that photography and the portrait in particular are never wholly liberatory vehicles of agency, nor unilateral instruments of subjugation. These images' affective stasis registers their subjects' struggle to inhabit colonization as an ongoing wound of dispossession, while refusing to accept the impossibility of living blackness with dignity and respect. They are practices that create the possibility for *re-assemblage in dispossession*.

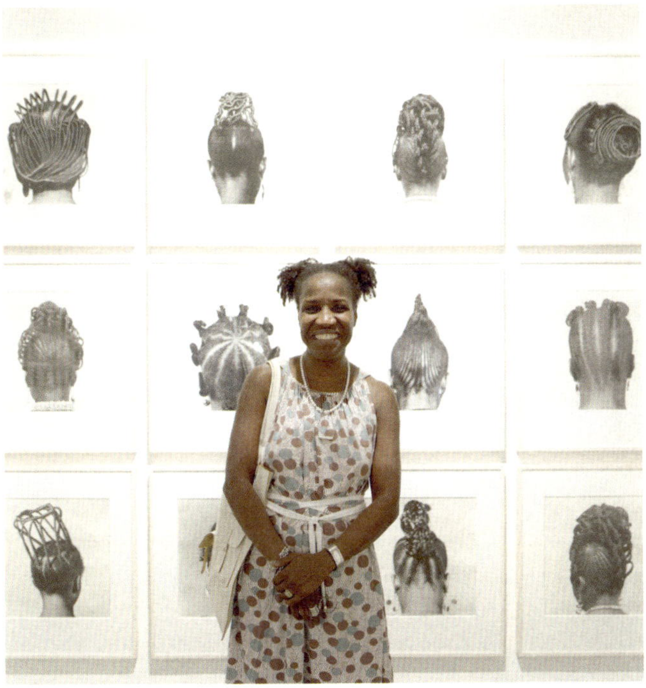

A day after viewing these images, I stood pondering an exhibit of J.D.'Okhai Ojeikere's stunning photos of Black women's hair and thinking about my encounter with the Mariannhill archive I had just seen. My reverie was interrupted by a delighted Dutch visitor who wanted to photograph me in front of Ojeikere's images. But she didn't really want to photograph me, she wanted to photograph my hair. "It's perfect," she exclaimed. "It's like having the real thing here!" I agreed to being photographed.

Confession #2: I hate taking photos. I freeze up and go rigid as a board. While I've learned to smile and sometimes even look like I enjoy them, tension permeates my body. When viewing images of myself, I feel something others do not. Perhaps I carry those affects with me in viewing the images of these five women. Probably, but then again, we all do. That's how affect works. It is what connects us to particular images and what makes our responses to them matter.

Alina Marazzi

SPECCHIO

MIRROR

Alina and the mirror of desires. Sense and sensibility in using archival images.

To speak of my affective relation with archival images—having to do not only with family photos, mine or other people's—I have to go back in time to the moment I found myself for the first time in front of the screen on which I was projecting fragmentary and uncertain frames of my mother's face, first as a child, then as a girl, and finally as a woman. A woman who at that time, more or less 15 years ago, persisted in being of my same age and whose face appeared on the screen as in a phantasmatic mirror that also reflected an ideal image of my own face blending with that of my mother, who had passed away 30 years earlier. It was with that first gaze into the mirror, through that encounter, comparison and identification, that I started to develop—at that time unknowingly—my own personal poetics in relation to the use of archival materials.

It all began with a family movie—which later was to be titled *Un'ora sola ti vorrei* (For one more hour with you, 2002)—made of films shot in 9½mm, 16mm, and 8mm by my maternal grandfather: the film represented the process of recapturing my personal memories, on the basis of which I created my own private family-cinematic lexicon, using the materials called *homemovies*. While making *Un'ora sola ti vorrei*, I sharpened my poetics, which I further developed in the films I made afterwards: *Vogliamo anche le rose* (We want roses too, 2007) and *Tutto parla di te* (All about you, 2012). As for my first film, it all came from within myself, from an internal need, or perhaps even from a certain limitation, due to the fact that in order to tell a story which was so dear to me, I had at my disposal "only" my family's amateur materials.

Un'ora sola ti vorrei triggered a dialogue between me and my mother, a dialogue that had been missing in real life, and which gained "body" and "voice" as I started to weave her life story on the basis of intimate and private materials such as *homemovies*, her letters and diaries. The need I had to encounter my mother 30 years after her death (she committed suicide in 1972 when I was 7) pushed me to browse in the family wardrobes and boxes in search of traces of her life and of my life as a child next to her. The encounter did take place, though not physically but emotionally and visually, the moment my face blended with hers—the face of a girl on the screen. Her words, which I kept reading over and over again until they

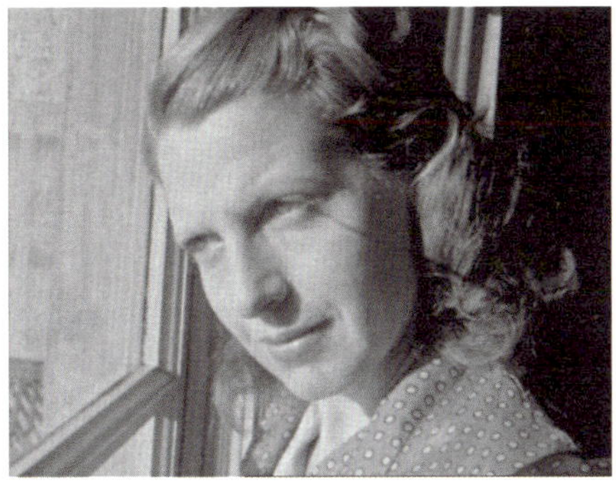

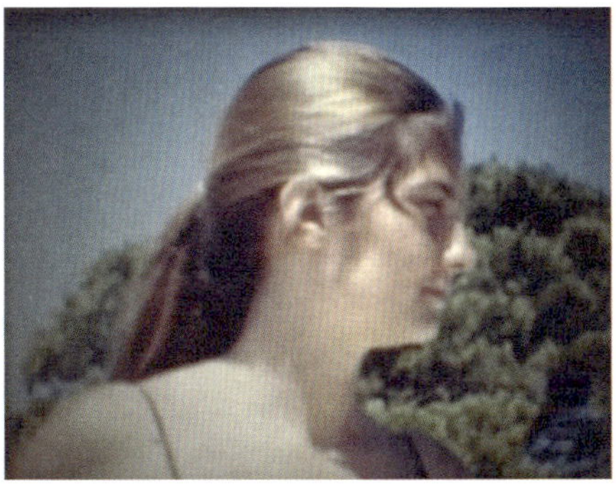

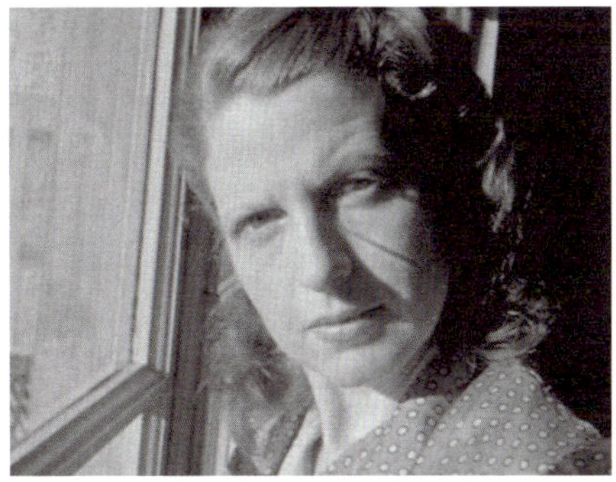

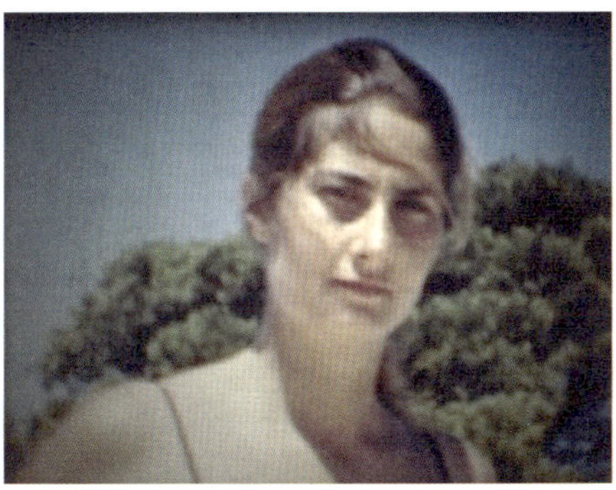

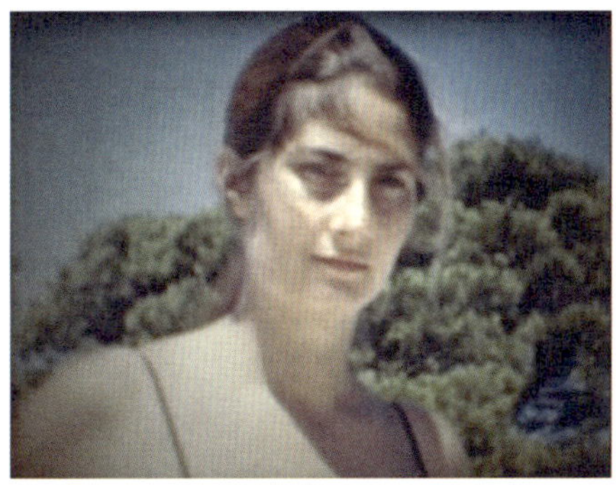

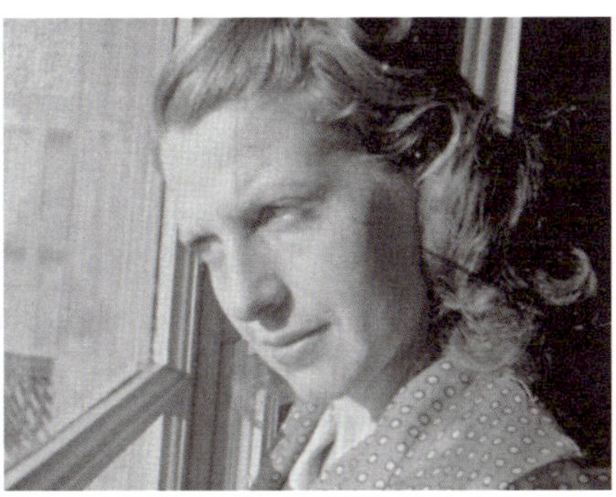

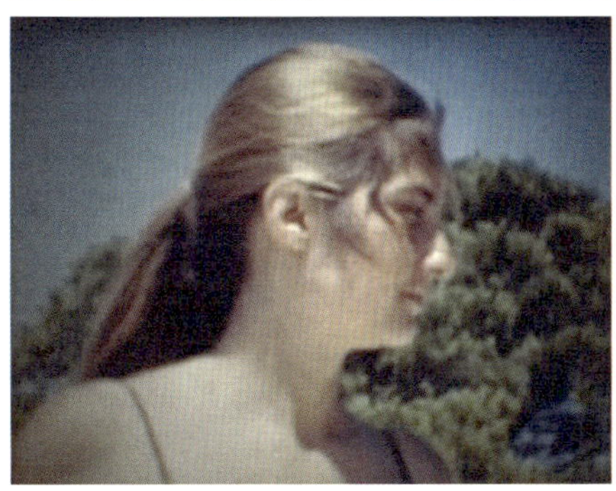

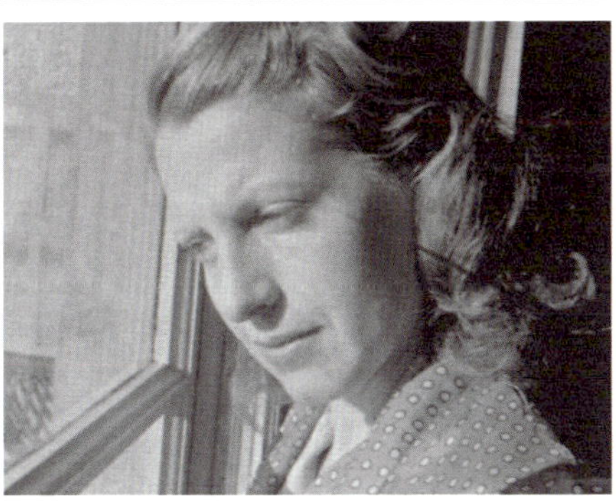

finally started to dwell within me, allowed me to say her name once again and suggest a possible relation between us. The film is narrated in the first person: the voice of Liseli, my mother, is actually my voice reading her words, while the face on the screen is the face of Liseli, but the gaze which brings her back to life in the space of the screen and in the time of the film, is my own. On the screen the entire space is occupied by Liseli's voice and image—a late compensation for her invisibility in real life; the space "around" the screen, however, is the space that I inhabit as the instigator and participant in this dialogue. If I had never looked at those images, no film would have existed.

In *Un'ora sola ti vorrei* I interrogated the very nature of *homemovies*, which aim to depict moments of private life always represented in their idyllic dimension; in the construction of my film narrative, however, those family images are "unveiled" to show also their dark side, taking on a function which differs from the classical function of *homemovies*. Through editing the earlier images are set free from their family dimension and take on a more purely filmic significance.

One example is the sequence in which I brought into relationship the gazes of two women, my mother's and my grandmother's. In the original black-and-white 16mm film dating back to the 1940s, Teresa, my grandmother, still young at the time, enters a room and walks up to a large window through which sunlight is streaming in, looks out, and then looks into the camera with a serious, almost sombre expression on her face, then she looks again in the distance, out of the window. In a standard colour 8mm film of the 1970s, my mother Liseli, at exactly the same age as her mother's, is shown on the beach in a medium shot, just like grandmother Teresa, in profile, her eyes looking out of the frame. Then she turns round and addresses a questioning and tired look towards the camera, in a posture similar to that of Teresa. In those *homemovies* both women, mother and daughter, are filmed in holiday resorts at different times, yet in similar postures and with similar expressions on their faces. The similarity between the frames of the black-and-white and the colour picture gave me the idea to associate them through editing, intercutting the black-and-white and colour shots, thus creating an exchange of looks between the two women. This technique is typical of classic film editing, where one connects characters by following the direction of their glances to create a sense of contact, to build an action, an emotion, or a story. This sequence shows the mother/grandmother as if she were giving her daughter a stern look. The daughter, in turn, "sensing" her mother's gaze, turns her head towards the camera and in this way virtually "encounters" her mother's look and returns it. The latter, though, in the next frame is shown while turning away and looking out of the window again, as though refusing to give her daughter the time needed for a real exchange of looks.

The meaning of this scene, created through editing, is my grandmother's rejection of the request for help expressed in the tired and worn gaze of my mother. The sequence is repeated twice in the film. By doing so, I wanted to stress that my mother, who was suffering from depression, was denied help by her own mother. It is, in a sense, a narrative trick made possible by editing: a choice I made as the director of the movie in order to talk about the lack of communication between Liseli and Teresa. All around this sequence my own look can also be felt, my way of seeing, which allows me to participate as a daughter in the two women's silent communication by means of a trans-generational mirror. At the same time, it enables me as a film director to talk about one aspect of their relation.

What's so attractive and appealing in family pictures is the sense of intimacy they convey and the strong relation between those who are taking them and those who are in front of the camera. Furthermore, the gap between the staging of everyday reality and its pretended casualness creates a tension, which is extremely fascinating both on an emotional and a filmic level. The uncertain and irregular process of amateur filming creates random "unnecessary" gaps in the narration, intervals which subtly unsettle the viewer. These gaps leave space for the viewers to slip into infiltrating it with their own family world; this is how we often identify with other people's *homemovies* when watching them. We search for similarities, compare those images with those that are, or could be, images of our own memories, or our memories themselves. This brings us close to the story we watch on the screen and gives us a sense of comfort as we feel part of a community.

Paolo Vignolo

TUMBAS

GRAVES

There are people who often go to the cemetery to visit their grandparents. There are some who have been there once only, for one of the many political funerals which are a tragic part of the Colombian experience. There are some who smoke marijuana with their dead, and there are others who have adopted an unnamed soul only to be able to communicate with the netherworld, and yet some others who practise white or even black magic. Activists of communist youth organizations remember their murdered comrades with *graffiti* painted with red varnish, mothers who buried their children when they were still small now bring them sweets and decals. Who knows how they imagine the afterworld. Revolutionaries might dream of it as the place of the red spring, where the sun of the future rises. For the mothers it is rather a sort of Disneyland inhabited by cartoon heroes and Baroque angels.

There are plenty of intermediaries: a guy dressed up as a priest, who, without permission from the Vatican, offers to celebrate a sung Mass for a few pennies, a lady offering to hire you a ladder to reach the funerary niches placed on higher levels, a guide offering his services to accidental tourists. Somehow, I am an intermediary, too, since I take my students here, and sometimes friends who come to visit me. So, if you feel like it, we can take a walk among the graves. Sometimes, if you want to understand the city of the living it is worth taking a look at the city of the dead.

On Monday the cemetery is at its most crowded. It is the souls' appointed day, when the boundaries between them and us become more porous and the communication with the afterworld is more intense. The sorrowful souls of purgatory and those suffering here on earth look for each other, exchange greetings, pleasantries, thanks or grumblings. Do you see the queue in front of this bronze statue, crouching like Rodin's *Thinker*? They are worshippers of Leo Kopp, waiting for their turn to beg for a job, whispering their words right to its ear. At the beginning of the twentieth century Leo Kopp was a powerful industrial tycoon of German origin. Today he is considered a patron saint of the jobless.

This is the tomb of Carlos Pizarro, a charismatic commander of the M-19 guerrilla group. Bunches of flowers covering the tomb almost hide a sword in low relief. It is Bolívar's sword, which the M-19 group stole in broad daylight, right in the centre of Bogotá in 1976. It was the first action of this guerrilla group, its political manifesto: "Bolívar is not dead. His sword cuts through the cobwebs of the museum and flings itself into the struggles of today. It is passed into our hands. Into the hands of armed people." 14 years later, just after he negotiated peace and came back to politics, Pizarro was murdered.

Many victims of drug and paramilitary violence are buried within the walls of this cemetery, from Luis Carlos Galán, a liberal, to communists such as Jaime Pardo Leal and Manuel Cepeda. Their tombs, however, are not so decorated with flowers. The reason is not political but religious: Pizarro became a saint. Popular devotion attributes to him miraculous powers, and that's why he is surrounded by ex votos expressing thanks for the graces they received. José Raquel Mercado, too, a trade unionist kidnapped by the same M-19 group, partakes in the aura of sainthood. The guerrilla group put him on trial for treason against the people and appealed to activists to vote, by means of street *graffiti*, whether to kill him or set him free. A few days later his body was found, riddled with bullets, in the trunk of a car. Today, a bust of Mercado, who was a black man from the port of Cartagena, has been adopted by the members of the Afro-Colombian community of Bogotá.

It is often quite difficult to say how it happens that someone comes to be worshipped. For instance, the most visited tomb is the one of Maria Salomé, an ordinary woman who died a violent death. She was a washerwoman and, as they say, a prostitute. To return the favour, a gentleman ordered to transfer her remains to the monumental part of the cemetery, where presidents, generals, poets, and dignitaries are buried. The place was literally transformed into a shrine ever since, a destination of pilgrimages undertaken to pay tribute to this working-class martyr, who performs miracles especially for those having problems with their sex life.

However, conflicts soon arose. The owners of the more expensive parcels complained with the city hall. This invasion by the rabble is unacceptable. They revere idols and practise rites that are contrary to the true religion. The sperm of their candles befoul our immaculate marble. They are dirty, uneducated. And, what is worse, they are poor. And we pay so much for our family mausoleums.

The situation became unbearable when the cult of Maria Salomé spread to the tomb of her neighbour, the renowned astronomer and mathematician Julio Garavito. In 1970 the International Astronomical Union named one of the craters on the Moon after him. On the dark side of the Moon, fair enough, but still on the Moon. Actually, we Colombians know him not so much because of his scientific achievements but because he is featured on the 20,000 peso banknote. Soon, the rituals performed in honour of Maria Salomé were addressed also to Garavito in the hope of getting financial assistance from one whose name was written on the Moon… and on the 20,000 peso banknote.

How is it possible, asked one of his relatives, that our dear dead Garavito lies next to a woman of ill reputation? And for all eternity! On the pretext of safeguarding property and avoiding too many visitors, the remains of Maria Salomé were transferred to a cemetery on the outskirts of the city. In a country where five million people were forced to flee their homes because of an armed conflict, who is going to worry about a dead woman expelled from her own grave? Yet the cult of Maria Salomé is stronger than ever. Mass pilgrimages followed the saint in exile, while another group of faithful still cherishes her memory in the central cemetery. Among the most ardent worshippers of Maria Salomé and Garavito is a group of transgendered prostitutes. A cemetery keeper told me, amused, that there was real confusion recently. One of the ladies, who received graces through the intercession of Garavito and was able to raise money for a breast implant, was so moved that she unbuttoned her blouse to show the saint the fruit of his miracle. Witnesses at the cemetery, shocked by this act of obscenity in a holy place, started to scream. The cemetery keepers, convinced it was a robbery, came running and started to fire their guns into the air. This is an everyday occurrence here. With all these padlocks, inspections, and constant brawls sometimes we feel we live in a prison. “It is not easy to keep law and order in the cemetery—the keeper admits—but it is my job. I am the soulkeeper.”

What is in fact the central cemetery in Bogotá? Is it an open-air museum, a shelter to hide from the chaos of the city, a prison for the souls, a place of commemoration of national tragedies? Perhaps one could see it as a great affective archive, both the *arkhé* through which we relate to our ancestors and the hierarchical city governed by archons. It reminds us that the one who controls the *necropolis* also rules the *polis*. But also that there comes a time when we have to come to terms with the life stories of the city of the dead. The affective charge hidden in this collective archive compels us to rethink the way we manage our traffic with the netherworld.

Ann Cvetkovich

EPHEMERA

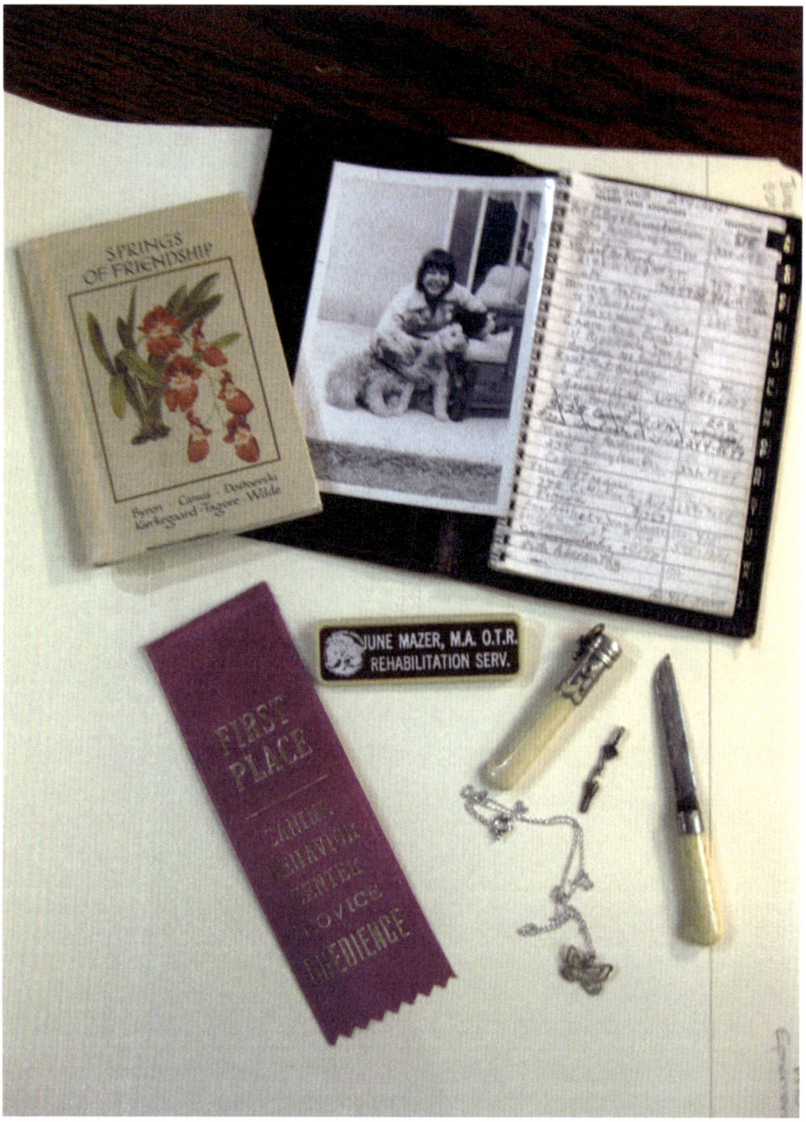
SPRINGS OF FRIENDSHIP
Byron · Camus · Dostoevski
Kierkegaard · Tagore · Wilde
JUNE MAZER, M.A. O.T.R.
REHABILITATION SERV.
FIRST PLACE

What happens when a grassroots lesbian feminist archive finds its way to the special collections of a major university research library? Does it lose its counterarchival aura, or can it carry its powers of critical intervention into new spaces? With these questions in mind, I arrived at UCLA (University of California, Los Angeles) to do research in collections from the June L. Mazer Lesbian Archives that have recently been housed and catalogued at the university as part of a partnership that began with digitizing some of the Mazer collections in order to make them more accessible. I have been following the collaboration for some time out of interest in how a new wave of queer collecting by universities and public libraries can transform archival practice.

The Mazer Archives emerged from the West Coast Lesbian Collections founded in Oakland, California in 1981 with the mission of collecting "anything a lesbian ever touched," a sensibility that also inspired Brooklyn's steadfastly independent Lesbian Herstory Archives. Faced with economic and logistical challenges, the collections were rescued in 1987 by June Mazer and Bunny MacCulloch, lovers and activists with a strong interest in archives, whose Altadena home was open for tours of the collections. In 1989, the archives were given space in a building donated by the city of West Hollywood and since then have been maintained primarily by dedicated volunteers; UCLA's resources are now giving them further stability.

On a previous trip, I had visited the Mazer's home base and appreciated its informal and welcoming atmosphere. This time, I wanted to see what it would feel like to access lesbian lives in a more conventional archive with its bureaucratic rules and regulations. Such visits sometimes require tedious advance preparation, including tracking through online finding aids and catalogues in order to figure out what boxes to request so that they can be retrieved from storage in time for your visit. It's very different from the community-based archives, where you can often roam the stacks freely, ask questions of volunteers who are deeply familiar with the collections, and browse buttons, posters, and other miscellany on display. Unlike the more impersonal reading rooms where special collections boxes are only available one folder at a time, the space itself becomes integral to the research. I decided to begin with June Mazer herself, whose name was given to the collections as a posthumous memorial in 1987. After her death, June's lover Bunny, an avid archivist, devoted her time to building and organizing the collections before her own premature death, also from cancer, in 1988, and it's possible that she assembled the two boxes of June Mazer materials.

When looking at queer archives, I gravitate towards ephemera, not just the occasional paper documents for which archivists use the term, but also the material artefacts that press up against the conventional boundaries of the archive and hint at ephemerality as that which escapes it. I was thus particularly intrigued by the following list in the finding aid:

"Box 2, Folder 1: Ephemera. 1970–78. Physical Description: small knife, jewelry, ribbon, two bound books."

I request the box with the ephemera but am mistakenly given Box 1 rather than Box 2 and thus begin with the more conventional overview of June's work as an activist and a professional. The paper documents bring to life her work as an occupational therapist, and I am intrigued to discover that she was interested in somatic approaches to healing, including a workshop called "Exploring How A Think Feels" [*sic*]. Scattered amidst the folders that contain copies of her article publications and workshop notes is personal correspondence, including love notes between her and Bunny. I pull out a batch of paper Valentines—the kind that children give each other in grade school. I carefully remove the coloured paper clip that holds them together and see that they are all from Bunny, who wrote funny messages inspired by the animal images on each one—"Leos love Crabs," says the lion. After spreading them out across the manila folder in order to take a photograph, I put them back as carefully as I can but little sparkles of glitter have been deposited on the bright orange paper provided by the library for taking notes. A queer form of archival dust, the glitter leaves a material trail of testimony to my intimate contact with June and Bunny's exchange.

As I make my way through the two boxes, there are many other discoveries that provide evidence of queer affects and intimacies. One folder contains a lengthy transcript of an astrology reading for June, who was a triple Cancer with "oceans of feeling." In addition to her involvement with drama therapy, June's creative activities included sketches of her domestic life with Bunny—their garden and hot tub, Bunny milking their pet goat, and their beloved cats and dogs. Things take a more sombre turn in the final folders, which document June's illness—medical records and caretaking logs, condolence letters from friends, receipts from her funeral, and more signs of dust—the plastic plaque that identified her ashes. Although it is sad to read of a life and love cut short, it is also in the lesbian feminist spirit of the Mazer to make this ordinary life special; by testifying not only to

June's accomplishments but to her daily activities, the boxes also make a case for the value of every lesbian life.

When I finally get to the ephemera folder, I take the silver butterfly necklace out of its tiny plastic bag, unsheathe the pearl-handled knife, open up the address book that includes a photo of June, and place them alongside the other objects to take a picture of the resulting collage. The mute objects and their odd juxtapositions speak to me, providing a sense of a life that lies beyond the folders. Personal and affective value is what matters in this mini-collection—the award ribbon for the beloved dog is as important as the name tag that represents June's professional status and the address book that reveals her wide circle of friends and contacts. Even though I can't really know what they mean, the necklace and the knife—gifts perhaps—no doubt represent other significant relationships and memories. To touch these objects is to receive a personal message from June about what she thought was important. Ephemeral objects have that power—gesturing to affective meanings that are attached to objects but not fully present in them, while also making immaterial ephemeralities material. Here in UCLA's Special Collections where I can only handle one folder and one box at a time, and where the materials thus remain sometimes quite literally remote, I am gratified to be able to touch the strange and random objects that have found their way into this space and thus feel that June Mazer's simultaneously humble and remarkable life still matters. As concrete as a pearl-handled knife, the ordinary lives of the lesbian feminist archive remain intact in the research library.

Ida & Henry Wilde (Keren Ida Nathan & Antonia Baehr)

GLOSS

GLOSS[1] (noun)

(ORIGIN mid-16th cent.: alteration of the noun ***gloze***, from Old French ***glose*** suggested by medieval Latin ***glossa* "explanation of a difficult word,"** and from Greek ***γλῶσσα*, *glōssa*, "word needing explanation"**)

Gloss is a brief marginal notation of the meaning of a word or wording in a text such as *glosses* in the margin: explanation, interpretation, exegesis, explication, elucidation; annotation, note, footnote, commentary, comment, and is typically found in a text as an appendix of specialized terms that a typical reader may find unfamiliar, or in the medieval legal tradition in which *glosses* were called *sedes materiae*: the seat of the matter, literally the very heart of the matter, which could be used to "explain away" misunderstandings or misinterpretations, to clarify and bring to light. On the other hand, to *gloss over* something has come to mean exactly the opposite of explaining something by pinning it down or letting it fly off the seat of a handle, since it means to cover over, to hide, to conceal or disguise, for example with make-up, costumes, or stories that aren't always true or untrue, and for example when wearing wilde costumes that have a certain gloss to them, you see, because then gloss begins to mean the shine or lustre on a silk cravat or the soft glow of a woollen blue stocking or indeed the sheen on the tweed weft of a well-cut waistcoat or the patina of a crisply ironed trouser leg, but especially like the glittering burnish of salmon-coloured satin underwear.

E.g.: "The *gloss*[2] wore off for Henry, after the first few months of living together because it was very different from a consumed marriage because Ida invented it so it was not like a play almost a real live play there were characters in it that Ida invented and we performed in it and anyone who came out of the extended kitchen. So it does have its real-life problems too. Like for example longing, because when Ida is not there, how to say, the happy years, the youth, when they lived together in the house, didn't last very long, because Ida had so many family members, that Henry couldn't cope with it. So then it became a fantasy, and it became about longing. You could call them the salmon days. The colour of Ida's underwear."
Henry Wilde (from an interview with Ida Wilde, 2013)

Ida Wilde

1 The word *gloss* was chosen for us by Uncle Mirjam, Henry Wilde's friend and Ida Wilde's third husband.

2 Here you have an example of the use of the word gloss as in "shine" (...the gloss wore off...), as well as the metatextual use of the verb to *gloss over*, as seen in the quotation by Henry Wilde, itself a text that glosses over the true story of the marriage of Ida and Henry Wilde. See book: *A Very Wilde Story; The True Story of the Marriage of Ida and Henry Wilde by Ida Wilde* (Kollektiv Tod Verlag and make_up Prod, 2014).

TIME IS PASSING CHAPTER I THE WILDE HAGGADAH a

The creation of the universe by a very ~~fat~~ little god

the first day there was coffee
the second milk
the third reading in bed.
the fourth linens
the fifth sewing
the sixth Henry
and on the seventh, the day of rest.
sex

Meine liebe Ida, 27.01.06

Time is passing and the winter is chilling cold and I realize this letter will never be finished. But letters should always stay unfinished, otherwise there is no way to send them out, because life is moving on and on and stories get old and dusty. Your Henry is not Marcel Proust but a construction worker who forgot about the linearity of time. You must see me: a real butch-man, a construction worker – but the hair will betray me, long and crazy like Einstein (Mirjam and me are using so much hair product due to your absence and our hirsute hippy-chap becoming that we have no known remedy to – or may be we enjoy watching the missing of you grown with our body hair...). However hair-time goes, life takes other meanders. There is construction-time which ~~goes~~ evolves very slowly and sturdily, with shelves, lamps and furniture-oil. There is dancing time with Werner for Petra, waiting for the "Feierabend-Bier" and half-happy time with a conceptual piece, watching the impossibility of my fellows to say "Werner, he" – so I became "hehe" or "hihi". Really a stuttering experience, this impossibility. I lacked in consistance with correcting the "she", especially of women calling me "Werner, she", and the group just couldn't make it inspite of a joyous atmosphere, or because of it.

Haggadah (noun) aramaic means "tales", "lore", "tel... "expanding", "binding" and ref... to the homiletic and non-lega... texts in the classical rabbini... literature of Judaism. It incorporates folklore, histo... anecdotes, moral exhortations practical advice from all sphe... of life, expanding understandin... while streghtening/binding beli...

...e creation of the ...iverse by a very ...ttle god
on the first day there was **coffee**
on the second **milk**
on the third **reading in bed**
on the fourth **linens**
on the fifth **sewing**
on the sixth **Henry**
and on the seventh, the day of rest **sex**

Time is passing and the winte... is chilling cold and I realize this letter will never be finis... But letters should always stay unfinished, otherwise t... is no way to send them out, because life is moving on and... and stories get old and dus... Your Henry is not Marcel Pro... but a construction worker w... forgot about the linearity of time.

(Mirjam and me are using ... much hair product due t... your absence and our hirsu... hippy-chap becoming that ... have no known remedy t... or may be we enjoy watchin... the missing of you grow wi... our body hair...). However hair-time goes, life takes other meanders.

...enesis (noun): origin, source, ...oot. Is the first book of the ...ntateuch. Its title in English, ...enesis" comes from the Greek of ... 2:4, "the book of the generation" ... title in the Jewish Scriptures ... the opening Hebrew word, ...reshit, "In the beginning."

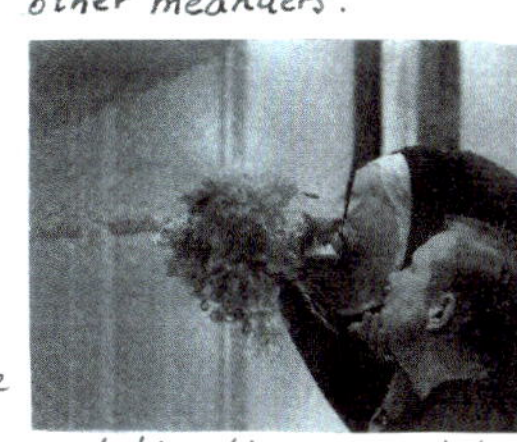

watching the impossibility of my fellows to say "Werner, he" – so I became "hehe" or "hihi".

...nry Wilde is known to some ... Werner Hirsch and to others ... Antonia Baehr and Henri Fleur.

"Dear Ida
Once more dear Ida"
– G. Stein

your husband Henry,
die alte ~~Rakete~~
Rakete"

FORMA

Guillermo Velasco • Zeichnung • Mischtechnik auf Papier
18.12. - 28.12.2010

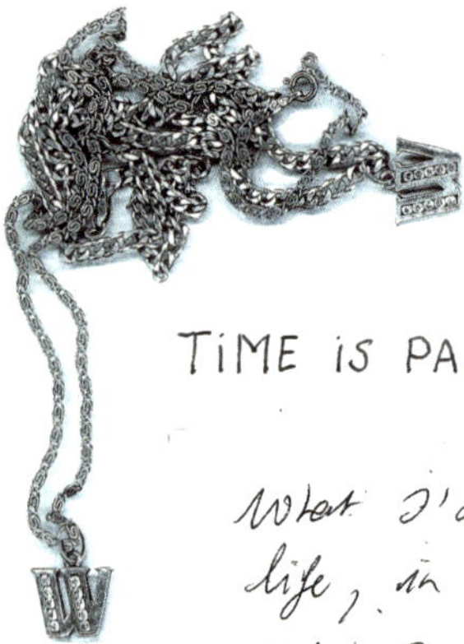

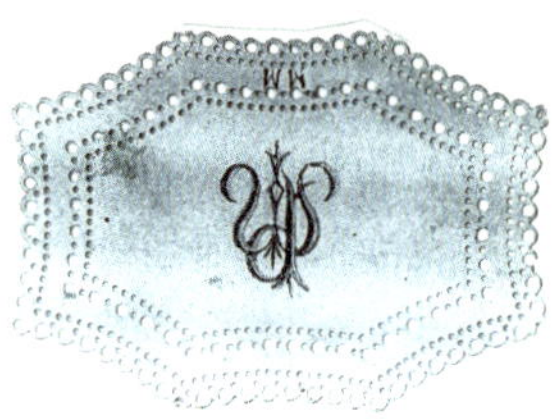

TIME IS PASSING CHAPTER I THE WILDE HAGGADAH

Mrs. Ida and Mr. Henry Wilde and Uncle Mirjam and Angie, the running reporter lived together happily in the house in Frankfurter Allee until December the 5th 2005 when Ida moved to Palestine and Henry moved to new lodgings in Wrangelstrasse in Berlin.

What I've always dreamt of: living above the busy life, in a tree, like "The baron in the trees" (Calvino) when I read that book as a little girl, I tried to do it for real, but my poor sportive abilities didn't allow me to realize that dream until now – in a more clappish way – in a warm appartment with shiny wooden floors I adore so much I almost ~~like~~ lick them all day long (the fetishist!) Henry the baron in the urban tree. But social life is also diffrent, more intense in a way when then I go down meet the friends. I see N. more often now (she lives alone too!) – she gave me new gentleman's perfume so my depravation slows down inspite of my ~~growing~~ hair: I still smell well! Today was a turn in life, with the new bed.. because since Stockholm I was quite sad, unsettled, restless, a bit lost. The appartment wasn't finished at all. Dust and paint everywhere. Just a matraze, no cosyness, no morning coffee, and you know how difficult that is for me. Still the Schrank doesn't fit in the appartment and it became a funny obsession. Funny dreams, like a limb of mine is still reaching out the door like Alice when she's so big she can't ~~put~~ her arm into the house. That Schrank is a part of my body, "goddamn"! But A. , Mirjam and E., my dear friends, have complete understanding for my queer situation and will come back with blankets and cords to get the Schrank in – a second try. I tell you, what a story!

Fetishist: (noun) with a twist. Is a one who licks wooden floors all day and kisses the feet of his lovely wife and loves his schrank. A fetish is an object that stands for/symbolizes god.

Fetishist is one who attaches sexual significance to an object.

"goddamn": Henry and uncle Mirjam pronounce it as "goddammen", which amuses Ida very much, since the "n" is actually silent.

Schrank: (noun) Old high German (scranc) a tall wardrobe-like German chest with double doors, constructed so as to partially dismantle for transport to the matrimonial home.

My dear wife Ida!

Many thousand thanks for your Henry in an armchair! When your husband will have become as fat as this Norwegian opera singer, he'll fit into the jacket. So long, he's just kissing the floor before your lovely feet.

(drawing)

(the portrayal of your very lovely legs failed a bit, i apologize)

many ♡ your henry

Willkommen zurück

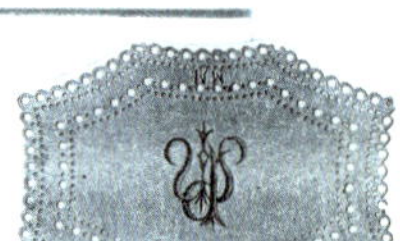

für meine liebe Ida ♡

dein Henri von Wilde

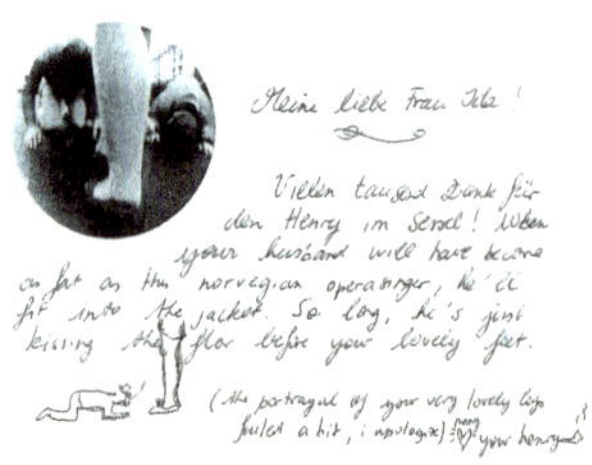

Meine liebe Frau Ida!

Vielen tausend Dank für den Henry im Sessel! When your husband will have become as fat as this norwegian operasinger, he'll fit into the jacket. So long, he's just kissing the floor before your lovely feet.

(the portrayal of your very lovely legs failed a bit, i apologize) many your henry

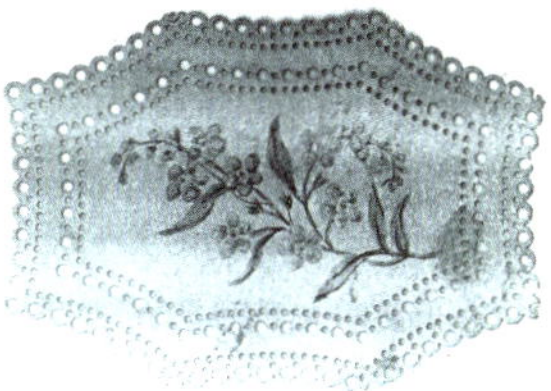

TIME IS PASSING CHAPTER I THE WILDE HAGGADAH c

Ida created Henry and then they were married and its an unconsumed marriage and Ida is only commenting on the margins and the Wilde family is grande and Uncle Mirjam is Ida's lover. And Henry has many others.

Oh! à propos old ladies! My mama, after a family disaster at my sister's, went to visit my grand-aunt G. (you know, the one who is always ajusting her big boobs as a tick, twice in a sentence). Well, she has demencia now and lives all by herself so she goes shopping "for the week-end" every day because she doesn't know what day it is. There is so much rotten food in her appartment that my mother had to carry out many trash bags. When Gunni saw the 40 cans of "Rollmobs"-Fisch, she said " quite coucou, no?"

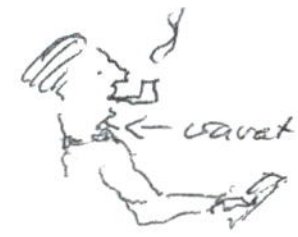

2006 was also the year, when uncle Mirjam fell back in love with the beautiful game of soccer and when after the bloody war in Lebanon uncle Mirjam and Ida became lovers again

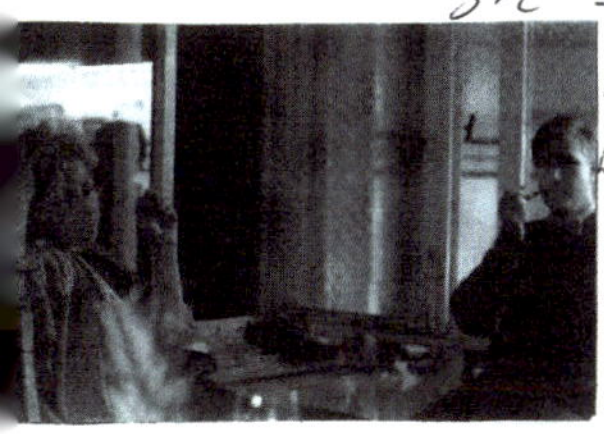

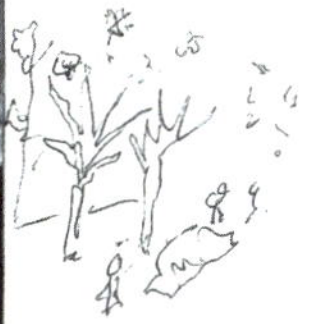

the trees and the cars and the people are all white in the snow storm below on Wrangelstrasse

Ida (quote) "We have to create more we can't reflect." 2014

I don't know. The whole thing was anyway all together quite amusing I must say, not dramatic in any way. The meander of time also brought about a swedish lesbian with glasses of shyness interviewing Ulf and me about Larry Peacock, presupposing we were a simple knitted drag-king group. The whole Dandy story quite unsettled her (you know, the double-twist in reappropriating masculinity that is already a conscious male construction, the dandy as you described him as the sun of his mother, not interested in sex, fetishist to the teeth, of good house). Then there was the presentation at Ausland of the choreographer Antonia Baehr to a bunch of international choreographers that went very well, because she presented all these artists she produces, and the female-dancers really understood the link.

The whole Dandy story quite unsettled her (you know, the double-twist in reappropriating masculinity that is already a conscious male construction, the dandy as you described him as the sun of his mother, not interested in sex, fetishist to the teeth, of good house).

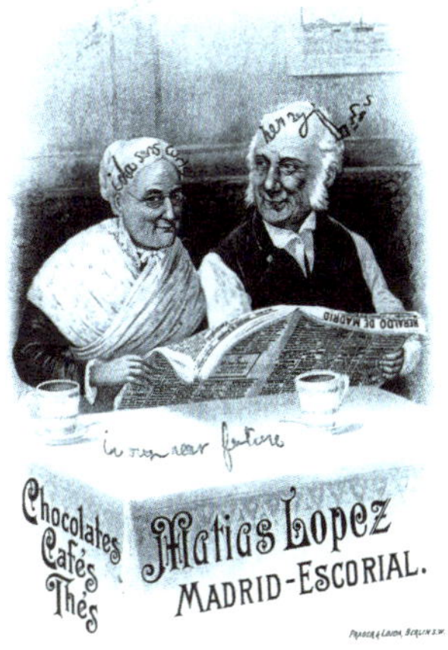

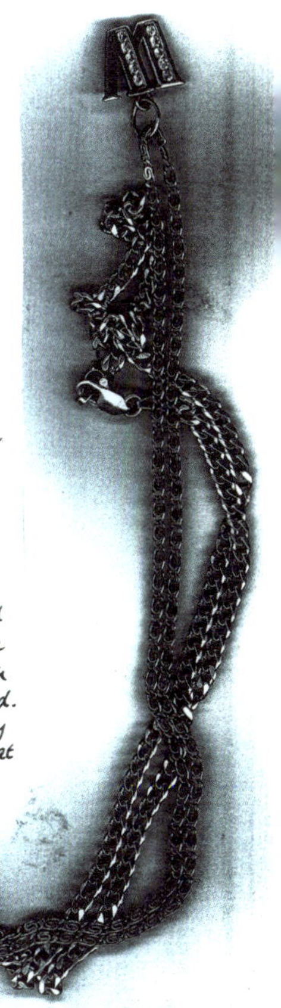

ida sans curls henry

ida sans curls henry
in our near future

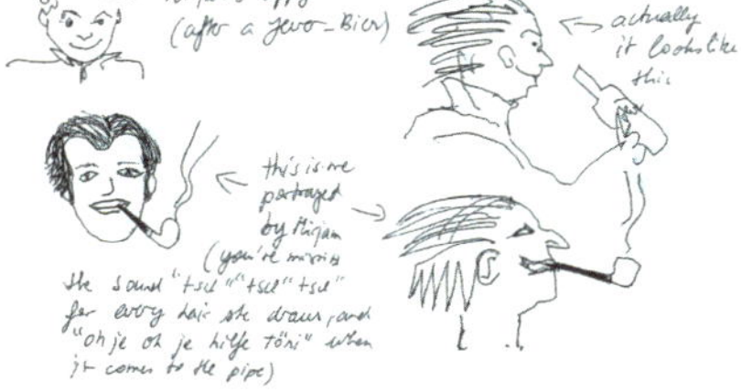

Now Henry sits in a café on the road to J.'s parents, wishing he would be at this table with you Ida, like you can see on the postcard from Madrid. This is exactly how you smile, my lovely one, "verschmitzt" – but what happened to your curles?

Forget me not (flower): In Lindy's piece "My Ulysses" there is a scene in which she reads a letter Henry Flower receives. Henry Flower is Leopold Bloom's pseudonym to write and receive love letters. There is a flower pinned to the letter. It ends with: "p.s.: what perfume does your wife use? I want to know." And everytime I thought of you... I was the dramaturge but I sat there every night making the titles. So I was in the piece without being in the lights for once and it was very nice. H.W.

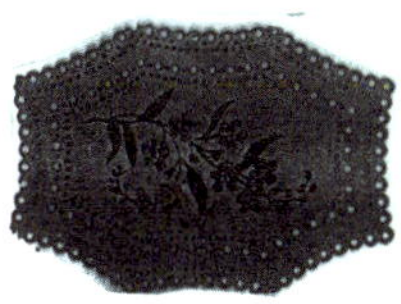

APPENDIX

Katarzyna Tórz

Katarzyna Tórz is the Head of Programming of the Polish Audiovisual Institute (NInA). She holds a Master's degree in philosophy from the University of Warsaw. She is currently working on her doctoral thesis at the Art Institute of the Polish Academy of Sciences. She has edited the books *Tak jakby nic się nie wydarzyło. Teatr Forced Entertainment* (2015), *Polityka wyobraźni. Scena flamandzka* (2011), and *Granice wykluczenia. Między etyką a estetyką / Limits of Exclusion: Between Aesthetics and Ethics* (2012) — the latter two with Dorota Semenowicz. She was the Associate Editor of *Leksykon Archiwum Afektywnego* (2015), the original version of *Lexicon for an Affective Archive*. She contributes to the Malta Festival in Poznań as a curator, developing the "Idioms" section of the programme.

Giulia Palladini and Marco Pustianaz

Giulia Palladini is a researcher in performance studies based in Berlin. She was Alexander von Humboldt fellow (2012–2014), and currently teaches at the Kunsthochschule Berlin-Weißensee. She has taught seminars as Guest Professor in various international institutions, such as the Universidad Nacional de Colombia in Bogotá and SNDO (School for New Dance Development) in Amsterdam. Her research focuses especially on performance labour and free time, the archive, and materialist theories of artistic production. Her texts appeared in several international journals, and she has collaborated as theorist and curator in a number of critical and artistic projects (e.g. *Affective Archives*, Vercelli 2009; *Living Rooms*, L'Aquila 2011; *Taking Time*, Helsinki 2013; *Experimenta / Sur*, Bogotá, 2014; *Zu ICH um WIR zu Sein*, Leipzig, 2014). Her book, *The Scene of Foreplay: Theater, Labor, and Leisure in 1960s New York*, will be published by Northwestern University Press in July 2017.

Marco Pustianaz is Associate Professor of English and Theatre at Università del Piemonte Orientale (Vercelli, Italy). Since the 1990s, he has been instrumental in the introduction of queer theory in Italy. He has co-edited *Generi di traverso* (2000) and *Maschilità decadenti* (2004) at the crossroads between literature, theory, cultural studies, gender and sexuality. More recently, he has focused on theatre and performance studies, working around the notion of affective archive. In 2010, he co-curated the international conference *Affective Archives* and co-edited its catalogue. He has published on queer theory, theatre affects, and the performance of spectatorship. He is editor of the book series Àltera (ETS, Pisa) devoted to a queer and gendered perspective on interculture.

The term "affective archive" was first employed in their common work in 2010, as the title of the Performance Studies international Regional Research Cluster *Archivi affettivi / Affective Archives*, which was organized in Vercelli (Italy) in collaboration with Annalisa Sacchi.

REFERENCES

Caruth, Cathy. "Unclaimed Experience: Trauma and the Possibility of History." *Yale French Studies: Literature and the Ethical Question*, vol. 79, 1991, pp. 181–92.

Derrida, Jacques. *Archive Fever: A Freudian Impression*. University of Chicago Press, 1996.

Felman, Shoshana. "Fire in the Archive: The Alignment of Witnesses." *The Future of Testimony: Interdisciplinary Perspectives on Witnessing*, edited by Antony Rowland and Jane Kilby, Routledge, 2014, pp. 48–68.

Kelleher, Joe. "On Self-Remembering Theatres", www.jonathanburrows.info/#/text/?id=18&t=content. Accessed 10 October 2016.

Pustianaz, Marco et al., editors. *Archivi affettivi / Affective Archives: A Catalogue*. Mercurio Edizioni, 2013.

Alessandra Violi

BOXES

Alessandra Violi is Full Professor of English Literature and Culture at Università di Bergamo (Italy), where she coordinates the PhD program in Intercultural Humanities Studies and the research group "Punctum," which is dedicated to the study of the image in a multidisciplinary key. Her research work has focused on the medical imaginary, especially on hysteria as a memory theatre (*Il teatro dei nervi*, 2004), on archives of affect (*Impronte dell'aria*, 2008; *Giocattoli*, ed., 2010) and on states of suspended animation ("Dead *pro tem*.", in *Monstruous Anatomies*, 2015).

REFERENCES

Caws, Mary Ann, editor. *Joseph Cornell's Theatre of the Mind: Selected Diaries, Letters and Files*. Thames and Hudson, 1993.

Benjamin, Walter. "One-way Street." *Selected Writings. Volume 1: 1913–1926*, edited by Marcus Bullock and Michael W. Jennings, Harvard University Press, 1996, pp. 444–88.

Benjamin, Walter. "Toys and Play." *Selected Writings. Volume 2, Part 1: 1927–1930*, edited by Michael W. Jennings et al., Harvard University Press, 1999, pp. 117–21.

Josipovici, Gabriel. *Hotel Andromeda*. Carcanet, 2014.

Scanlan, John. *On Garbage*. Reaktion Books, 2005.

Simic, Charles. *Dime-Store Alchemy: The Art of Joseph Cornell*. NYRB Classics, 2011.

Steedman, Carolyn. *Dust*. Manchester University Press, 2001.

IMAGE CAPTIONS AND CREDITS

p. 22 Smithsonian Institution Archive, unknown photographer, photographic print. © Smithsonian Institution Archive, reprinted with permission.

p. 23 Old box, unknown photographer.

p. 24 Joseph Cornell's cellar workshop, photograph by Hans Namuth, 1969. © Hans Namuth Ltd Photography, reprinted with permission.

P. 25 *Mybox*, photograph by Richard Davies. Reprinted with permission.

Kateřina Šedá

VNUĈKA

GRANDDAUGHTER

translated by Iván Gutiérrez

Kateřina Šedá lives and works in Brno-Líšeň, Czech Republic. She studied at the Academy of Fine Arts in Prague. In her actions, which she often implements in the countryside or the suburbs, Šedá tries to establish bonds among the local people. With the aid of their own (provoked) activities and the unconventional use of everyday resources, she attempts to arouse a permanent change in their behaviour. Šedá has exhibited internationally at such venues as SFMOMA, USA (2014); the Venice Biennale, Italy (2013); Tate Modern, London (2011); Documenta 12, Kassel, Germany (2007) etc.

IMAGE CAPTIONS AND CREDITS

p. 29 Jana Šedá, *Je to jedno / It Doesn't Matter*, credits: Kateřina Šedá.

p. 32 Milada Šoukalová, *Normální život / Normal Life*, credit: Kateřina Šedá.

Dorota Krakowska

KRES

LIMIT

translated by Arthur Barys

Dorota Krakowska studied graphic design at the Kraków Academy of Fine Arts. She collaborated with Anna Bujnowska on the publication of *Szkice z pamięci* (2009) by Ewa Krakowska and on the exhibition *Byliśmy*, devoted to the Jews of Tarnów before World War II (2014, BWA Modern Art Gallery and the Regional Museum in Tarnów). Together with Wiola Sowa she produced *Endblum* (2014), a film that uses archival footage to tell the story of eastern European Jews before World War II. Her interests include printmaking, video installations and performance art. Her work has been displayed at solo exhibitions at Dansmuseet (Stockholm) and Zderzak Gallery (Kraków), and at group shows at the National Museum in Warsaw, Poznań and other venues. She has worked at the Kraków Goethe Institute's Programming Department since 2000.

IMAGE CAPTIONS AND CREDITS

p. 36 A page from a Hebrew language textbook found in a Kraków cellar.

p. 39 Prints from photographic plates left behind by an unknown man fleeing the war.

Rabih Mroué

WARNING

Rabih Mroué (Beirut) is an actor, director, visual artist, playwright, and contributing editor of both *Kalamon* (Beirut) and *TDR* (New York). He is one of the founding members of the executive Board of the Beirut Art Center (BAC). He was a fellow at the International Research Center "Interweaving Performance Cultures", Freie Universität Berlin. His work explores the responsibility of the artist in communicating with an audience in given political and cultural contexts, and includes *So Little Time* (2016), *Ode to Joy* (2015), *Riding on a Cloud* (2013), *33 tours et quelques secondes* (2012), *The Pixelated Revolution* (2012), *The Inhabitants of Images* (2008), and *Who's Afraid of Representation* (2005).

IMAGE CAPTIONS AND CREDITS

p. 42 Israeli leaflet dropped over Beirut in July 1982.

pp. 44–49 Photos of the leaflets reproduced with the author's permission.

Claudia Castellucci

ORDIGNO

DEVICE

translated by Marco Pustianaz

Claudia Castellucci was born in Cesena (Italy) in 1958. After studying at art college, she undertook a degree at the Academy of Fine Arts in Bologna. In 1981, she was a founding member of Socìetas Raffaello Sanzio, for which she has written both dramatic and theoretical texts. She has created "schools of rhythm," some devoted to the study of dance, others to the study of representation. She has published *Uovo di bocca. Scritti lirici e drammatici* (2000) and *Setta. Scuola di tecnica drammatica* (2015).

REFERENCES

Bloch, Ernst. *Spirit of Utopia.* Stanford University Press, 2000.

Warburg, Aby. *Per Monstra ad Sphaeram: Sternglaube und Bilddeutung,* edited by Davide Stimilli, and Claudia Wedepohl, Dölling und Galitz, 2008.

IMAGE CAPTIONS AND CREDITS

pp. 54, 57 Illustrations reproduced with the author's permission.

p. 55 *Historic Device* (2014), 6 ink drawings embedded into velvet pages folded concertina-like. Size (when closed): 30.5 cm × 20 cm. Height: 10 cm.

p. 56 *Memorial Column* (2014), 14 ink drawings embedded into the plinth and capital of a heptagonal column (wood, velvet). Plinth and capital width: 50 cm. Shaft width: 30 cm. Height: 250 cm.

Franz Anton Cramer

BEWEGUNG

MOVEMENT

translated by Michelle Miles

Franz Anton Cramer is Lecturer at the Department for Studies in Music and Dance at Paris Lodron University Salzburg, Austria. Between 2003 and 2008, he collaborated with the Leipzig Dance Archives, the Centre National de la Danse and the Bibliothèque-Musée de l'Opéra de Paris in a project investigating dance in the 1930s and '40s. He has promoted an initiative to federate several German dance documentation centres between 2008 and 2012 as part of *Tanzplan Deutschland.* Together with Barbara Büscher, he is co-editor of the special-interest magazine *MAP — Media | Archive | Performance* (www.perfomap.de).

REFERENCES

The archives of Pierre Tugal can be consulted online at the Centre National de la Danse's website: http://inventaire.cnd.fr/ → théoriciens, écrivains, critiques et autres personnalités → Pierre Tugal. Accessed 10 October 2016.

Baxmann, Inge, et al., editors. *Les Archives internationales de la danse 1931 à 1952.* Centre National de la Danse, 2006.

Cramer, Franz Anton. *In aller Freiheit. Tanzkultur in Frankreich zwischen 1930 und 1950.* Parodos, 2008.

Wimmer, Mario. *Archivkörper. Eine Geschichte historischer Einbildungskraft.* Konstanz University Press, 2012.

Elisabeth Lebovici

SIDA

AIDS

translated by William Bishop

Elisabeth Lebovici is an activist and art critic based in Paris who worked as an arts editor for the newspaper *Libération* from 1991 to 2006. Her blog is at http://le-beau-vice.blogspot.fr. She co-organizes the bi-monthly seminar "Something You Should Know: Artists and Producers" at the École des Hautes Études en Sciences Sociales, Paris. She is the co-author, with Catherine Gonnard, of a history of women artists in France (*Femmes artistes, artistes femmes: Paris, de 1880 à nos jours*, 2007). *Ce que le sida m'a fait: art et activisme à la fin du XXè siècle* will be published in 2017 (JRP|Ringier-Les amis de la Maison Rouge). She is a member of the research group "Travelling Féministe" around the Centre Audiovisuel Simone de Beauvoir, Paris.

REFERENCES

1858 videos of Lionel Soukaz can be seen at:

http://www.dailymotion.com/soukaz. Accessed 10 October 2016.

You can also find:

http://vimeo.com/74418469: *Carottage* (extracts from the video journal). Accessed 10 October 2016.

http://vimeo.com/74961466: Lionel Soukaz films Michel Journiac's performance *150 poèmes mis en sang*. Accessed 10 October 2016.

http://vimeo.com/74105607: Lionel Soukaz, *RV Mon ami*. Accessed 10 October 2016.

http://vimeo.com/75373143: Lionel Soukaz, *Copi Je t'm*. Accessed 10 October 2016.

Journiac, Michel. http://www.journiac.com. Accessed 10 October 2016.

Labaume, Vincent, and Emmanuel Guigon, editors. *Michel Journiac*. Editions des musées de Strasbourg, 2004. Catalogue.

Watney, Simon. *Practices of Freedom, Selected Writings on HIV/AIDS*. Duke University Press, 1994.

Bettina Knaup

RECOMBINATIONS

translated by Michelle Miles

Bettina Knaup works internationally as a curator with a focus on performance and gender. She has been co-curator of the International Festival of Contemporary Arts—City of Women, Ljubljana, and has contributed to the performing arts laboratory "In Transit" at Haus der Kulturen der Welt, Berlin. Recent projects include *performance platform. body affects* (with S. Bake at Sophiensaele, Berlin, 2012) and *re.act.feminism #2: A Performing Archive*, a growing and travelling archive project curated with B. E. Stammer (Akademie der Künste Berlin; Antoni Tàpies Foundation, Barcelona; Wyspa, Gdańsk, etc., 2011–2013).

REFERENCES

Appadurai, Arjun. "Archive and Aspiration." *Information is Alive: Art and Theory on Archiving and Retrieving Data*, edited by Joke Brouwer and Arjun Mulder, NAi Publishers, 2003, pp. 14–25.

Fabião, Eleonora. "Performing Feminist Archives." *reactfeminism # 2*, edited by Bettina Knaup and Beatrice Stammer, Verl. für Moderne Kunst, 2014, pp. 29–36.

Hemmings, Clare. *Why Stories Matter: The Political Grammar of Feminist Theory*. Duke University Press, 2011, p. 129, emphasis added.

Birbragher, Francine, editor. *In Body and Soul: The Performance Art of María Teresa Hincapié*. Patricia & Phillip Frost Art Museum, 2010. Catalogue.

Knaup, Bettina and Beatrice E. Stammer, editors. *re.act.feminism # 2: A Performing Archive*. Verl. für Moderne Kunst, 2014. For further information, see also http://www.reactfeminism.org. Accessed 10 October 2016.

Ukeles, Mierle Laderman. *Manifesto of Maintenance Art*, 1969, http://www.feldmangallery.com/media/pdfs/Ukeles_MANIFESTO.pdf. Accessed on 10 October 2016.

Erik Göngrich

EINMACHGLAS

PRESERVE JAR

Erik Göngrich is an artist working in the public space by using various methodologies, including collaborations, exhibitions, guided tours, photographs, building, and cooking sessions. His projects are the result of long research periods, and he is especially interested in investigating images of the city and the history of places. His artistic interventions in urban spaces aim to transform the way we look at or experience and use particular places: his sculptural objects transform places fallen out of use, abandoned or damaged into spaces of public exchange and communication. His artistic work is about history, trust, political space, modern architecture, cooking, and sculpture.

More information can be found at www.goengrich.de

REFERENCES

The photos/drawings in this publication are from Kolomna (Russia) and Havana (Cuba), the places I like to refer to.

La creatividad está aquí—Creativity is here was a drawing performance in the public space of La Playa / Havana (Cuba), 2014.

Kolomna 1991 – Kolomna 2014 was an exhibition with photos from two different times at Artkommunalka in Kolomna (Russia) in 1991 and 2014.

BIOCUB explored how a single person or a whole family can live from drying fruits. The exhibition happened during the 11th Havana Biennial in collaboration with LASA—Laboratorio Artístico de San Agustín—in Havana (Cuba), 2012.

NUMBERS was a performance that numbered with a brush and white paint the public space of Kolomna in 1991.

IMAGE CAPTIONS AND CREDITS

p. 78 "Performing / living / cooking / dancing with and in the Communal-Flat-Museum: Art Kommunalka", Kolomna/Russia (a town 113 km south of Moscow), July 2014.

p. 79 "Let's salute the 56th Anniversary of the triumph of the Revolution with better service." 56 years of preserved revolution in Havana/Cuba, November 2014.

p. 80 "Russian eggs are called in America deviled eggs and in France oeuf mimosa". Bottled eggs in Kolomna/ Russia, 2014.

p. 91 Home bottling museum.

Zdenka Badovinac

CARDBOARD BOX

translated by Barbara Skubic

Zdenka Badovinac is a curator and writer, who has served since 1993 as Director of the Moderna Galerija in Ljubljana. In her work, Badovinac highlights the difficult processes of redefining history alongside different avant-garde traditions in contemporary art. Badovinac's first exhibition addressing these issues was *Body and the East—From the 1960s to the Present* (1998). She also initiated the first eastern European art collection, "Arteast 2000+". Badovinac was Slovenian Commissioner at the Venice Biennale from 1993 to 1997 and in 2005, Austrian Commissioner at the São Paulo Biennial in 2002, and the President of CIMAM (International Committee for Museums and Collections of Modern Art), 2010–13.

REFERENCES

Badovinac, Zdenka. *Prekinjene zgodovine :arteast razstava = Interrupted histories.* Moderna Galerija Ljubljana, 2006.

De Baere, Bart, and Christian Höller. *L'Internationale. Post-War Avant-Gardes Between 1957 and 1986.* JRP|Ringier, 2013.

Annemarie Mieke Matzke / She She Pop

SCHUBLADEN

DRAWERS

translated by Michelle Miles

Annemarie Mieke Matzke is Professor of Experimental Forms of Contemporary Theatre at the University of Hildesheim (Germany), as well as a founding member of the German performance collective She She Pop. She is a graduate of the Institute for Applied Theatre Studies in Giessen, and holds a doctoral degree from the Freie Universität Berlin. Her publications include a recent monograph, *Arbeit am Theater: Eine Diskursgeschichte der Probe* (2012), and a number of co-edited collections of essays (*Das Buch der Angewandten Theaterwissenschaft*, 2012, among others).

She She Pop is a performance collective founded in the late 1990s by graduates of the Applied Theater Studies program in Gießen. Members are Sebastian Bark, Johanna Freiburg, Fanni Halmburger, Lisa Lucassen, Annemarie Matzke, Ilia Papatheodorou, and Berit Stumpf.

Schubladen (2012)

Devised by: She She Pop

Realized by: Sebastian Bark, Johanna Freiburg, Barbara Gronau, Annett Gröschner, Fanni Halmburger, Alexandra Lachmann, Katharina Lorenz, Lisa Lucassen, Annemarie Matzke, Peggy Mädler, Ilia Papatheodorou, Wenke Seemann, Berit Stumpf and Nina Tecklenburg.

REFERENCES

Bataille, George. "The Notion of Expenditure". *Visions of Excess. Selected Writings 1927–1939*, edited by Allan Stoekl, University of Minnesota Press, 1985, pp. 116–29.

Flusser, Vilém. *Dinge und Undinge: phänomenologische Skizzen*. Carl Hanser, 1993.

Mauss, Marcel. *The Gift: The Form and Reason for Exchange in Archaic Societies*. Routledge, 2002.

IMAGE CAPTIONS AND CREDITS

All pictures are from the performance *Schubladen* (2012).

p. 90 Photographer Ayako Abe.

p. 93 Photographer Benjamin Krieg.

Tim Etchells

INDEX CARDS

Tim Etchells is an artist and writer whose work shifts between performance, visual art, and fiction. He has been leader of the world-renowned Sheffield-based performance group Forced Entertainment since its inception, and is currently Professor of Performance at Lancaster University. In recent years, he has exhibited widely in the context of visual arts, combining solo shows, group shows, and commissioned projects for public sites. Recent publications include *Vacuum Days* (2012) and *While You Are With Us Here Tonight* (2013).

For more information see: www.timetchells.com

REFERENCES

Etchells, Tim. *Endland Stories: Or Bad Lives*. Pulp Faction, 1998.

Etchells, Tim. *Certain Fragments: Contemporary Performance and Forced Entertainment*. Routledge, 1999.

Etchells, Tim. *The Broken World*. Windmill Books, 2009.

Etchells, Tim. *Vacuum Days*. Storythings, 2012.

Etchells, Tim. *While You Are With Us Here Tonight*. Live Art Development Agency, 2013.

IMAGE CAPTIONS AND CREDITS

pp. 97, 99 Index cards from the performance *A Broadcast / Looping Pieces* (2014), reproduced with the author's permission.

Paul Clarke
STEWARD

Paul Clarke is an artist, theatre director, and Senior Lecturer in Performance Studies at the University of Bristol. From 2008 to 2010, he was Research Fellow on the project *Performing the Archive: The Future of the Past*, hosted by University of Bristol's Live Art Archives and the Arnolfini archive; following this he was a co-investigator on the AHRC-funded *Performing Documents* project. He directs the theatre company Uninvited Guests, whose work has toured nationally and internationally, and is a member of the art collective Performance Re-enactment Society (PRS).

REFERENCES

Borggreen, Gunhild, and Rune Gade, editors. *Performing Archives / Archives of Performance*. Museum Tusculanum Press, 2013.

Freeman, Elizabeth. *Time Binds: Queer Temporalities, Queer Histories*. Duke University Press, 2010.

Heathfield, Adrian, and Amelia Jones, editors. *Perform, Repeat, Record: Live Art in History*. Intellect, 2012.

National Review of Live Art Video Archive: https://dedefi.ilrt.bris.ac.uk/. Accessed 10 October 2016.

Performing Documents project website: http://www.bristol.ac.uk/arts/research/performing-documents/. Accessed 10 October 2016.

Schneider, Rebecca. *Performing Remains: Art and War in Times of Theatrical Re-enactment*. Routledge, 2011.

IMAGE CAPTIONS AND CREDITS

p. 104 Jess Robins, one of Arnolfini's invigilators, performing *Group Show* (2012), photo by Carl Newland.

Małgorzata Szczęśniak
BIEL
WHITENESS

translated by Arthur Barys

Małgorzata Szczęśniak is a practitioner and theoretician of psychology, set design, and photography. A long-time collaborator of director Krzysztof Warlikowski, Szczęśniak has also co-authored numerous opera and theatre productions on stages across Europe.

IMAGE CAPTIONS AND CREDITS

pp. 114–121 Photographs reproduced with the author's permission.

Małgorzata Dziewulska

DRZAZGI

SPLINTERS

translated by Arthur Barys

Małgorzata Dziewulska has been developing a personal archival project focusing on theatre testimonies in order to excavate the affective nature of the exchange between stage and audience. The archive is at once a repository for the testimonial documentation of the collective imagination with its historical, social, and political content.

She is the author of the books *Teatr zdradzonego przymierza* (1985), *Artyści i Pielgrzymi* (1995), and *Inna obecność* (2009). She has worked as a university lecturer and as literary director of major theatres in Warsaw and Kraków, and has directed several operas. Her current interests include documentary filmmaking. Małgorzata Dziewulska works with the Instytut Teatralny (Theatre Institute) in Warsaw, where she runs a seminar on Tadeusz Kantor.

IMAGE CAPTIONS AND CREDITS

p. 125 Funeral procession for the casualties in the fire of the travelling cinema in Wielopole.

p. 125 Newspaper cutting found in Szufnarowa memorial chamber.

p. 125 A makeshift schoolhouse housed in army barracks.

The author wishes to thank Roman Lipa's family and Eliza Siulborska (Institute of Ethnology and Anthropology, Warsaw University).

Graeme Miller

IMMEMORIAL

Graeme Miller is an artist, whose work emerges from performance in the 1980s and 1990s, co-founding the influential Impact Theatre Co-operative and making his own stage work that includes *A Girl Skipping* (1990). He now works across a range of media and contexts—from video to sculpture, and from gallery to landscape. His work is often compositional, may include a leading element of audio, and frequently returns to geographical ideas. These include *Linked* (1993), *The Sound Observatory* (1992), *Bassline* (2004–2009), *Track*, (2010), *On Air*, (2012), and his ongoing installation, *Beheld*, (2006–).

REFERENCES

Artsadmin, www.artsadmin.co.uk/artists/graeme-miller. Accessed 10 October 2016.

Artsadmin, www.artsadmin.co.uk/projects/linked. Accessed 10 October 2016.

Linked by Graeme Miller. A Landmark in Sound, an Invisible Artwork, a Walk, www.linkedm11.net. Accessed 10 October 2016.

Wishart, Sarah. "Archive — Remembering the M11 protests and Graeme Miller's 'Linked'", www.sarahwishart.co.uk/research/remembering-the-m11-protests-and-graeme-millers-linked/. Accessed 10 October 2016.

IMAGE CAPTIONS AND CREDITS

p. 132 Linked transmitters, 2014, image by Graeme Miller.

p. 134 Olympic Velodrome, London, 2014, image by Graeme Miller.

Heidi & Rolf Abderhalden / Mapa Teatro

TESTIGOS

WITNESSES

translated by Claudia Espinosa Johnson

Mapa Teatro is an artist-run laboratory dedicated to transdisciplinary creation based in Bogotá, and founded in 1986 by Heidi, Elizabeth, and Rolf Abderhalden, Colombian artists of Swiss origin. In recent years, Mapa Teatro has particularly focused on the production of artistic events at the crossroads between micro-politics and poetics, through the construction of ethno-fictions and the temporary creation of "experimental communities." Mapa Teatro has spawned artistic experimentation processes in different locations and platforms investigating Colombian reality: it thinks of itself as a laboratory of social imagination. Among their most recent works are *Testigo de las ruinas* (2002–2012); *Los santos inocentes* (2010); *Discurso de un hombre decente* (2011); *Los Incontados: un tríptico* (2014).

Rolf Abderhalden is the founder and current director of the Interdisciplinary Master Program in Theatre and Live Arts of the Universidad Nacional de Colombia, in Bogotá and Barranquilla.

IMAGE CAPTIONS AND CREDITS

p. 140 Antanas Mockus, Juana María Ramírez in *Testigo de las ruinas / archivo vivo*, lecture-performance, SF MOMA, 12 December 2012, photo by Rolf Abderhalden.

canecapovolto & Elisa Abela

CONDOMINIO

CONDOMINIUM

translated by Marco Pustianaz

canecapovolto group was formed in Catania (Italy) in 1992. Continuously experimenting in various media including acoustic films, videos, happenings, and collages, canecapovolto investigates the expressive potential of vision and the dynamics of perception, adopting original techniques for treating and manipulating images. Working from film sources, and making visual and sound experiments with super-8 shorts, the group draws on various audio-video production techniques, "sabotaging" the initial media image to catch viewers off-guard. A great deal of attention is paid to the critical examination of scientific communication models and to viewer-response analysis.

Since 2008, **Elisa Abela** has been a musician active in the independent rock scene as a guitar player in Joe Lally's band. She started her own artistic research by collaborating with canecapovolto in the exhibitions *Presente Continuo* and *Diwan*. Although she has experimented with various media—from photography to oil painting—most of her current production focuses on graphic works on paper. She also creates collages, drawing from her long-lasting passion for old publications, such as illustrated news magazines, children's books, manuals, school notebooks, family photographs, newspaper and magazine advertisements.

REFERENCES

canecapovolto website: www.canecapovolto.it. Accessed 10 October 2016.

canecapovolto videos: www.vimeo.com/canecapovolto. Accessed 10 October 2016.

canecapovolto audioworks: https://soundcloud.com/canecapovolto. Accessed 10 October 2016.

canecapovolto Facebook page: www.facebook.com/canecapovolto. Accessed 10 October 2016.

IMAGE CAPTIONS AND CREDITS

pp. 144–147 All images © canecapovolto & Elisa Abela, reproduced with the authors' permission.

Paola Di Cori

VOLVER

RETURN

translated by Hanna Szulczewska

Paola Di Cori was born and raised in Buenos Aires and lives in Rome. She has been Lecturer and Visiting Professor at the universities of Harvard, London, Sydney, Buenos Aires. She taught Cultural Studies and Gender Studies at the University of Urbino (Italy) until her retirement in 2009, and has published extensively on gender history and theory, historiography, and cultural studies. She has co-edited *Rovine future* (2010) and is the author of a book on Italian feminism (*Asincronie del femminismo*, 2012). She has also written extensively on Michel de Certeau, and was one of the founders in 2009 of the homepage www.micheldecerteau.eu.

REFERENCES

Aciman, André. *Harvard Square.* Norton, 2013.

Molloy, Sylvia. *El común olvido.* Buenos Aires, Norma, 2002.

Naipaul, V. S. *The Enigma of Arrival.* 1987. Macmillan, 2011

Sebald, Winfried Georg. *The Emigrants.* New Directions, 2016 .

IMAGE CAPTIONS AND CREDITS

p. 153 Photographs reproduced with the author's permission.

Joe Kelleher

UNANSWERED

Joe Kelleher is Professor of Theatre and Performance at Roehampton University, London. He is the author of *Theatre & Politics* (2009), co-author with Claudia and Romeo Castellucci, Chiara Guidi, and Nicholas Ridout of *The Theatre of Socíetas Raffaello Sanzio* (2007), and co-editor with Nicholas Ridout of *Contemporary Theatres in Europe* (2006). His latest book, *The Illuminated Theatre: Studies in the Suffering of Images*, was published by Routledge in May 2015. In recent years, he has been making occasional performance duets with Eirini Kartsaki.

REFERENCES

Foster, Hal. "An Archival Impulse." *October*, vol. 110, Fall, 2004, pp. 3–22.

Ricoeur, Paul. *Memory, History, Forgetting.* Translated by Kathleen Blamey and David Pellauer, University of Chicago Press, 2004.

Tina Campt
STASIS

Tina Campt is Claire Tow and Ann Whitney Olin Professor of Africana and Women's, Gender and Sexuality Studies, and Director of the Barnard Center for Research on Women at Barnard College, Columbia University. She is the author of three books: *Other Germans: Black Germans and the Politics of Race, Gender and Memory in the Third Reich* (2004), *Image Matters: Archive, Photography and the African Diaspora in Europe* (2012), and *Listening to Images* (2017).

REFERENCES

Campbell, James T. "African Subjects." *The Black Photo Album / Look at Me 1890–1950*, edited by Santu Mofokeng, Steidl, 2013.

Fanon, Frantz. *The Wretched of the Earth*. Translated by Constance Farrington, Grove Press, 1963.

Rippe, Christoph. "'Histrionic Zulus'—Photographic Heterotopias at the Catholic Mission Mariannhill in Natal." *Safundi: The Journal of South African and American Studies*, vol. 15, no. 2&3, 2014, pp. 179–96, http://dx.doi.org/10.1080/17533171.2014.925649. Accessed 10 October 2016.

Scott, Darieck. *Extravagant Abjection: Blackness, Power and Sexuality in the African American Literary Imagination*. New York University Press, 2010.

IMAGE CAPTIONS AND CREDITS

p. 162 Collection Museum of Ethnology, Leiden (RV-A15-9, RV-A15-19, RV-A15-41, RV-A15-45, RV-A15-54).

p. 165 Tina Campt, photo by Mariette Aernoudts, MD FotoArt, www.mdfotoart.nl.

Alina Marazzi
SPECCHIO

MIRROR

translated by Hanna Szulczewska

The main body of **Alina Marazzi**'s work is her film trilogy on female subjectivity, motherhood, and memory: *Un'ora sola ti vorrei* (2002), *Vogliamo anche le rose* (2007), and *Tutto parla di te* (2012) (the latter starring Charlotte Rampling). The first uses personal home movies to explore the life story of her deceased mother. The second investigates the lives of Italian women during the sexual revolution in the 1970s by engaging a dialogue with archival footage, underground and private home movies. The last portrays the ambivalence of maternity by intermingling a variety of visual languages, such as fiction, documentary, photography, stop motion. She investigates the relationship between film and cultural identity through a gendered perspective based on women's biographical experiences, and interrogates the role played by "technologies of memory," thus problematizing the nature of found footage and archival material.

REFERENCES

Cantin, Maristella, editor. *Italian Women Filmmakers and the Gendered Screen*. Palgrave, 2013.

Luciano, Bernadette, and Susanna Scarparo. *Reframing Italy: New Trends in Italian Women's Filmmaking*. Purdue UP, 2013.

Sabbadini, Andrea, editor. *Projected Shadows, Psychoanalytic Reflections on the Representation of Loss in European Cinema*. Routledge, 2007.

Tutto parla di te pressbook: www.intramovies.com/catalogue/details.php?id=571&dn=pressbook_en.pdf. Accessed 10 October 2016.

Vogliamo anche le rose website: http://www.vogliamoanchelerose.it. Accessed 10 October 2016.

Wilson, Emma. *Love, Mortality and the Moving Image*. Palgrave, 2012.

IMAGE CAPTIONS AND CREDITS

p. 169 Stills reproduced with the author's permission.

Paolo Vignolo
TUMBAS
GRAVES

translated by Hanna Szulczewska

Paolo Vignolo is Associate Professor of History and Humanities at the National University of Colombia, Bogotá. His fields of research and creative exploration deal with public history, cultural heritage and memory studies, play, live arts, and festive performance. He holds a Ph.D. in History at the École des Hautes Études en Sciences Sociales (E.H.E.S.S.) of Paris, and actively collaborates with the Hemispheric Institute of Performance and Politics at New York University and with the Cultural Agents Initiative at Harvard University.

Website: unal.academia.edu/PaoloVignolo.

REFERENCES

Certeau, Michel de. *The Writing of History*. Translated by Tom Conley, Columbia University Press, 1988.

Colectivo Vividero. *Proyecto Márgenes*. Part 1: *Acción de Gracia*, and Part 2: *Canciones para vivos y muertos*, www.vividerocolectivo.com. Accessed 10 October 2016.

Derrida, Jacques. *Archive Fever: A Freudian Impression*. University of Chicago Press, 1996.

Erlick, June, editor. "Memory: In Search of History and Democracy." *Re-Vista. Harvard Review of Latin America*, vol. XIII, no. 1, Fall 2013, http://revista.drclas.harvard.edu/files/revista/files/revista_f13_ship_spreads_revise.pdf?m=1410443346. Accessed 10 October 2016.

Grupo de Memoria Histórica. *¡Basta ya! Colombia: memorias de guerra y dignidad*. Centro Nacional de Memoria Histórica, 2014, www.centrodememoriahistorica.gov.co/micrositios/informeGeneral/descargas.html. Accessed 10 October 2016.

Vignolo, Paolo. "¿Quién gobierna la ciudad de los muertos? Políticas de la memoria y desarrollo urbano en Bogotá", *Memoria y Sociedad, Políticas de la memoria y usos públicos de la historia*, vol. 17, no. 35, July–December 2013, pp. 125–42. Download site: revistas.javeriana.edu.co/index.php/memoysociedad/article/download/8332/6758. Accessed 10 October 2016.

Ann Cvetkovich
EPHEMERA

Ann Cvetkovich is Ellen Clayton Garwood Centennial Professor of English and Professor of Women's and Gender Studies at the University of Texas at Austin. She is the author of *Mixed Feelings: Feminism, Mass Culture, and Victorian Sensationalism* (1992); *An Archive of Feelings: Trauma, Sexuality, and Lesbian Public Cultures* (2003); and *Depression: A Public Feeling* (2012). She co-edited (with Ann Pellegrini) "Public Sentiments," a special issue of *The Scholar and Feminist Online*, and (with Janet Staiger and Ann Reynolds) *Political Emotions* (2010). She has been co-editor, with Annamarie Jagose, of *GLQ: A Journal of Lesbian and Gay Studies*. Her most recent writing projects focus on the current state of LGBTQ archives and their creative use by artists to make counterarchives and interventions in public history. She is also exploring the concept of the sovereignty of the senses.

Website: www.anncvetkovich.com

REFERENCES

Cvetkovich, Ann. *An Archive of Feelings: Trauma, Sexuality, and Lesbian Public Cultures*. Duke University Press, 2003.

Cvetkovich, Ann. "Photographing Objects as Queer Archival Practice." *Feeling Photography*, edited by Elspeth Brown and Thy Phu, Duke University Press, 2014, pp. 273–96.

June Mazer Lesbian Archives website: http://www.mazerlesbianarchives.org. Accessed 10 October 2016.

June L. Mazer Lesbian Archive at Department of Special Collections, Charles E. Young Research Library, University of California, Los Angeles, http://digital2.library.ucla.edu/mazer/, Accessed 10 October 2016.

June L. Mazer papers, 1929–1988 (Collection LSC 2136). UCLA Library Special Collections.

McHugh, Kathleen A. et al. *Making Invisible Histories Visible: The June L. Mazer Lesbian Archives, A Resource Guide to the Collections*. UCLA Center for the Study of Women, 2014.

IMAGE CAPTIONS AND CREDITS

p. 180 Ephemera from June L. Mazer Papers, Box 2, Folder 1: Ephemera, 1970–78, photograph by Ann Cvetkovich, by permission of June Mazer Lesbian Archives and UCLA Special Collections.

Ida & Henry Wilde (Keren Ida Nathan & Antonia Baehr)
GLOSS

Ida Wilde is Henry Wilde's wife and was born at the London University Hospital in the last century. In her spare time, Ida is also known to some as Keren Ida Nathan: author, director, librettist, lyricist, and landscape painter. In Berlin, Ida met Henry, and the rest is history, now to be seen in a glossy new illustrated edition of the book, *A Very Wilde Story; The True Story of the Marriage of Ida and Henry Wilde* (2014). One can order the book on the Make Up Production's website and learn more about Ida on www.fara-films.net/Keren-Ida-Nathan-Ida-Wilde.

Henry Wilde is Ida Wilde's husband and a gentleman dandy. In his spare time he is also known to some as the horse whisperer and dancer Werner Hirsch, the choreographer and filmmaker Antonia Baehr, and the musician Henri Fleur, amongst others. You may find out more about him, the Wilde's, and all the glossy branches of the family on the website: www.make-up-productions.net.

IMAGE CAPTIONS AND CREDITS

Gloss, text by Ida Wilde.

pp. 187–189 "The Wilde Haggadah" (2014), original text and artwork by Ida Wilde and Henry Wilde, black/white collage, 3 pp.

First published in the UK in 2017 by
Intellect
The Mill, Parnall Road, Fishponds
Bristol, BS16 3JG
UK

First published in the USA in 2017 by
Intellect, The University of Chicago Press
1427 E. 60th Street
Chicago, IL 60637
USA

Co-published with NInA (http://www.nina.gov.pl/) and
the Live Art Development Agency (www.thisisliveart.co.uk)

A catalogue record for this book is available from the British Library.

The editors would like to acknowledge the financial support of the University of Roehampton's Department of Drama, Theatre and Performance.

Copy-editor: MPS Technologies
Cover designer: Błażej Pindor
Typesetting: Błażej Pindor
Production manager: Katie Evans

Printed and bound by
Drukarnia Argraf, Poland.

This is a peer-reviewed publication.

Print ISBN: 978-1-78320-778-7

ePDF ISBN: 978-1-78320-779-4

Live Art Development Agency

University of Roehampton London

NATIONAL AUDIOVISUAL INSTITUTE NInA